791.43 Manchel, Frank
Ma
        Gangsters on the
        screen

SALK JR. HIGH MEDIA CENTER
ELK RIVER, MN 55330

GANGSTERS ON THE SCREEN

GANGSTERS ON THE SCREEN

BY FRANK MANCHEL

FRANKLIN WATTS • NEW YORK • LONDON • 1978

Cover design by Neil Stuart

*Photographs courtesy of the
Lester Glassner Collection.*

Library of Congress Cataloging in Publication Data

Manchel, Frank.
    Gangsters on the screen.

    Bibliography: p.
    Includes index.
    SUMMARY: Surveys the gangster genre of movies and possible effects of movie violence on audiences.
    1. Gangster films—History and criticism—Juvenile literature. 2. Moving-pictures—United States—Juvenile literature. 3. Violence in motion pictures—Juvenile literature. [1. Gangster films—History and criticism. 2. Motion pictures. 3. Violence in motion pictures] I. Title.
PN1995.9.G3M35   791.43'0909'352   78-5953
ISBN 0-531-01471-1

Copyright © 1978 by Frank Manchel
All rights reserved
Printed in the United States of America
5 4 3 2 1

CONTENTS

- **SEA OF BLOOD**
  1
- 1898–1929 • **BREEDING GROUNDS**
  9
- 1929–1934 • **HEADLINE HEROES**
  27
- 1935–1939 • **SWITCH**
  42
- 1940–1949 • **A NEW TRADITION**
  52
- 1950–1959 • **THE SYNDICATE YEARS**
  70
- 1960–1969 • **LOST BOUNDARIES**
  84
- 1970–1978 • **STRICTLY BUSINESS**
  96
- **BIBLIOGRAPHY**
  114
- **INDEX**
  116

FOR STEVEN

From a proud father to a wonderful son who has given me more joy than anyone has a right to expect.

OTHER BOOKS BY FRANK MANCHEL

Movies and How They Are Made

When Pictures Began to Move

When Movies Began to Speak

Terrors of the Screen

Cameras West

Film Study: A Resource Guide

Yesterday's Clowns: The Rise of Film Comedy

The Talking Clowns: From Laurel and Hardy to the Marx Brothers

An Album of Science Fiction Films

Women on the Hollywood Screen

GANGSTERS ON THE SCREEN

MICHELLE PHILLIPS
AND WARREN OATES
IN *DILLINGER*

SEA OF BLOOD

The gangster film is famous for its violence and action-packed stories. Born out of a unique American experience, it has become one of Hollywood's most popular and most original gifts to the world of movie fiction.

Today the gangster film is enjoying a spectacular rebirth. Movies dealing with notorious bandits, thieves, syndicate mobsters, assassins, bank robbers, and killers are everywhere in the seventies. Some notable examples are *The Godfather, Dillinger, The Valachi Papers, The Friends of Eddie Coyle, The Getaway, The Mechanic, Lucky Luciano, Dog Day Afternoon, Crazy Joe,* and *The French Connection.*

The current fascination with crime stories is also evident on television. Every night the national pastime is to watch Kojak, Pepper, Baretta, Barnaby Jones, Columbo, Charlie's Angels, or Starsky and Hutch protect helpless citizens from mayhem and murder. The tough cops, the private eyes, and the undercover agents of TV are familiar visitors in our living rooms at night.

What worries many critics is the effect that these movies and TV serials are having on audiences. Opponents of screen violence claim that Starsky and Hutch, for example, teach us to tolerate violence; Baretta provides a classroom for criminal techniques; and Kojak fosters aggressive behavior. Such popular lawmen, the ar-

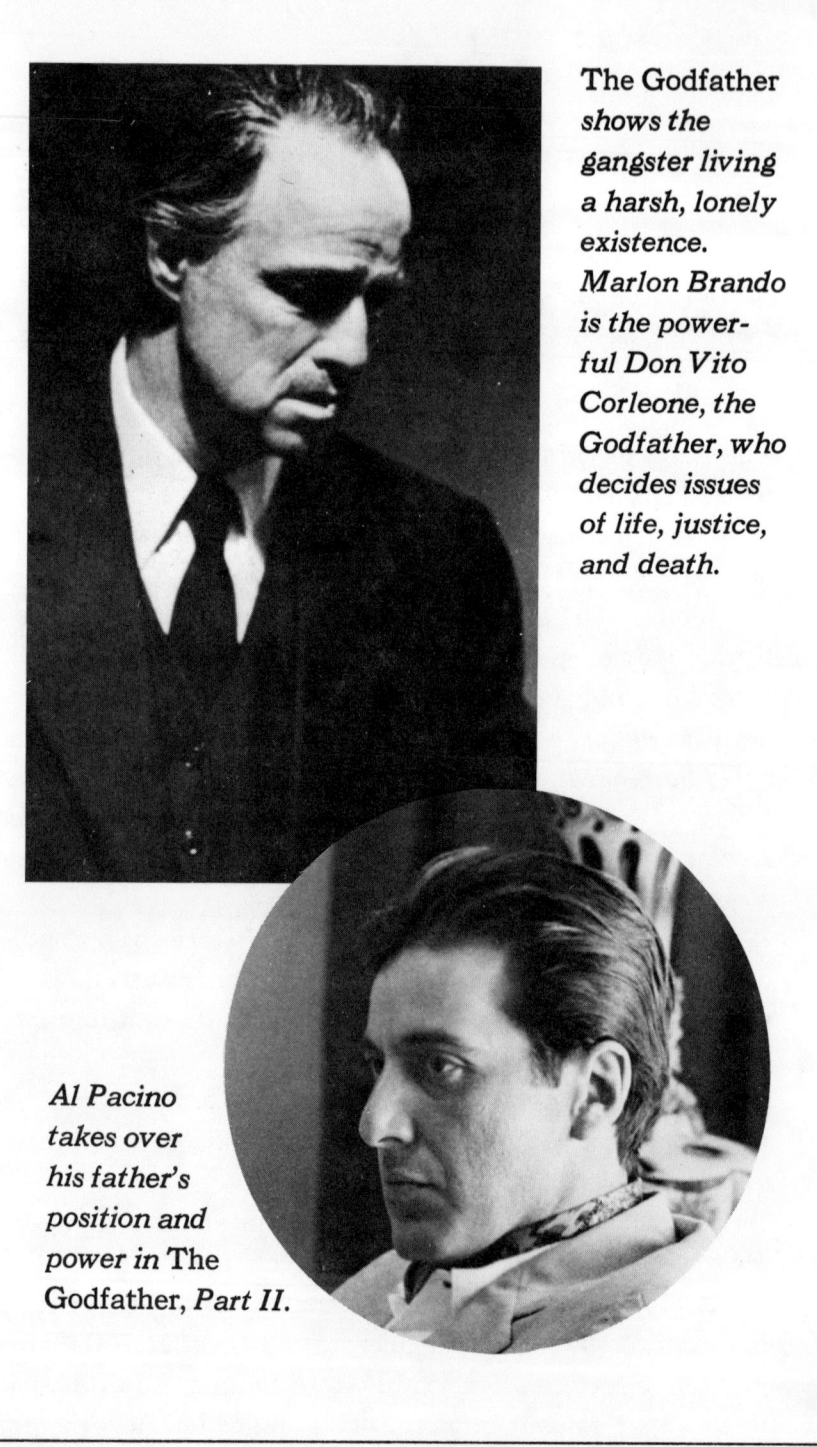

The Godfather *shows the gangster living a harsh, lonely existence. Marlon Brando is the powerful Don Vito Corleone, the Godfather, who decides issues of life, justice, and death.*

Al Pacino takes over his father's position and power in The Godfather, Part II.

gument goes, help make us insensitive to human suffering and encourage the belief that force is the best answer to our problems.

To support their claims, critics point to over a thousand studies of TV violence and behavior that suggest the bad effects blood-and-guts stories have on audiences. In 1970, for example, The National Commission on the Causes and Prevention of Violence concluded that "violence on television . . . fosters moral and social values about violence in daily life that are unacceptable in civilized society." Two years later, the U.S. Surgeon General's Scientific Advisory Committee felt its findings required the need for "immediate and remedial action." Reporting to Congress, the nation's highest ranking medical officer stated, "The overwhelming consensus [is] that televised violence does have an adverse effect on certain members of society." Most social scientists support the Surgeon General's verdict and are now trying to identify what types of children are affected by violent programs and under what conditions.

The news media have been quick to inform the public of sensational cases. One instance involved a fourteen-year-old Columbus, Ohio, youngster who accidentally killed his kid brother with a gun as the two boys innocently imitated a scene from the movie *Dirty Harry*. Another case concerned the murder of a former Vermont state prison inmate who had been garroted (strangled from behind with a length of wire) during the run of *The Godfather*. Still another example dealt with a fifteen-year-old Miami boy who murdered an elderly woman during a robbery attempt and later claimed he was "inspired" by an episode on *Kojak*. Most sensible critics, however, realize that drawing general conclusions from such isolated cases would be a mistake. But the examples do show that films and TV can affect behavior.

What worries the critics is the fact that Americans, regardless of age, cannot ignore the scenes of violence on their TV screens. (One study concluded that the average fifteen-year-old youngster had witnessed approximately 13,400 video murders.) As a result, pressure groups like the national Parent-Teacher Association started a grass-roots campaign to force the TV industry to reduce its crime shows. In 1977, the PTA was joined by the American Medical Association, which claimed that TV violence was "both a mental-health problem and an environmental issue." Always quick to react to pressure, TV producers canceled police shows like "Ironsides," "S.W.A.T.," "The Rookies," "McCloud," "Macmillan," and "The Streets of San Francisco."

Those who defend the violent screen offer compelling arguments. First they unveil scientific studies sponsored by the TV industry that dispute the theory that screen violence and antisocial behavior are tied closely together. What's more, the defense claims that studies like the U.S. Surgeon General's Report have been misrepresented. David Gerber, the producer of "Police Story" and "Police Woman," reminds critics that the 1972 Report was not a document unanimously agreed upon by the committee's members, and that it also contained the statement, "children who show aggressive tendencies can *possibly* be motivated by aggressive situations on TV, but if so, they already have a bent for it."

At the same time, the defense attacks the motives—conscious or subconscious—of its critics. History has shown, they point out, that every new technological development in human communication has faced the wrath of pressure groups worried about public morality. Concerned individuals have issued similar warnings about the printing press, the nickelodeon, the silent films, the talkies, comic books, radio, and now TV. According to Gerber, the

Peter Falk (left) as Lt. Columbo gave criminals the fake impression he was a bumbling fool, while really being a brilliant investigator. As Sgt. Pepper Anderson, Angie Dickinson offers an exciting image of a female crime fighter on Police Woman.

Above: in Little Caesar, *Edward G. Robinson portrayed Caesar Enrico Bandello, the two-bit hood who became an underworld big shot. Below: James Cagney starred as the tough guy in* The Public Enemy. *Mae Clarke demonstrated that being a gangster's moll was a hard life.*

pressure groups "use the TV violence issue as an excuse ... for avoiding the great issues that face this country."

A third defense argument is that the use of violence in entertainment and art predates movies and TV. Blood-guts-and-brutality have formed a crucial part of art, from the ancient Greek tragedies through Elizabethan drama and up to contemporary times. Frank Price, president of Universal Television, the studio leader in TV production, offers no apologies for "Starsky and Hutch," "Police Story," "Kojak," and "Baretta." In his eyes, they are well-done shows, and, he says, "We've got the Emmys to prove it."

The defense also argues that screen violence is true to life. *Super Fly* shows that people become criminals because of poverty, racism, and ignorance. *The Valachi Papers,* based on a real-life case, explains that organized crime makes most of its money by giving the public what it wants: desperately needed loans, narcotics, prostitutes, and gambling. *The Godfather* describes what the news media report daily, that crime corrupts government, destroys the weak, and adds to the lawlessness in society. To force creative people to be less honest in their crime stories is dangerous because it "sanitizes" violence. Viewers don't realize how horrible criminals really are. David Wolper, executive producer of "Roots," complains his famous show could not be made as realistically today because of the demand for less TV violence.

No matter what side you take in the debate, one central fact is clear. Gangster films have had a popular and controversial history. From their start at the turn of the century, crime stories have focused on the dark side of the American Dream. In the thirties, for example, films like *Little Caesar, The Public Enemy,* and *Scarface* mirrored the nation's anger and disillusionment during the Great Depression. In the sixties, movies like *Bonnie and Clyde,*

Madigan, and *Bullitt* reflected the social revolution against outworn traditions and corrupt institutions.

Everybody by now is familiar with the conventions of the gangster film. Test your memory with the following scenes:

• Machine gun bullets tear into a stoolie's stomach. Bleeding and screaming, he falls face forward into the gutter.

• During Prohibition days, a World War I veteran tells off his mobster brother: "You think I'd care if it was just beer in that keg? I know what you've been doing all this time . . . where you got those new clothes and those new cars—you've been telling Ma that you've gone into politics . . . that you're on the city payroll. YOU MURDERER! It's not beer in that keg! It's beer and blood. Blood of men!"

• A gangster returns to the slum area where he was born and becomes a hero to the local youth gang. Two boyhood friends who grew up on opposite sides of the law meet for a violent showdown. A punch-drunk, two-bit fighter decides to help the crime commission in its fight against the labor boss who rules the neighborhood.

The time is right to examine this popular genre. How accurate are its stories? What do they tell us about our country and ourselves? Who have been its famous creators and stars? What has been left out? How has the industry responded to its critics? What films have used violence artistically to reveal the art of moving pictures?

Obviously, this small book cannot answer these questions in great detail. Yet it can start you thinking about the violent world of the gangster movie. In any case, we will have a chance to get a much-needed historical look at one of the most disturbing issues facing us today.

The story of the Hollywood gangster is linked closely to the story of organized crime in America. It has been that way since the era of the movies began at the turn of the century. The tie-in was the result of an historical accident.

Movies started off as a toy, a novelty, a low-brow amusement. The well-to-do and the educated scorned the primitive films. The working class did not. Because poor people rarely left their neighborhoods, the movie pioneers brought motion-picture shows to them. By 1900, hundreds of empty rooms had been made into makeshift storefront theaters in America's big-city slums.

Crime proved to be one of the most popular film subjects. *The Burglar on the Roof* (1898) made fun of a clumsy crook. *A Career of Crime* (1902) showed in five different episodes how a man's criminal career began with a theft from a fruit stand and ended in the electric chair. *Rounding Up of the "Yeggmen"* (1904) reenacted the headline story of a recent bank robbery and showed how the crooks were captured by the police.

To understand why crime movies were so popular, we need to know who made up these early film audiences. Where did they come from? Why did they enjoy movies so much?

The early film audiences consisted largely of newcomers to America. They had been attracted by the young nation's stress on individualism and success. Like their ancestors, the immigrants had suffered from social, religious, and economic injustices. To these desperate and courageous people, America was the land of opportunity. All that was necessary for success, so they believed, was hard work, faith in God, and obedience to the nation's laws.

America insured its rapid growth by encouraging individualism. Business and capital had few restrictions placed on them. Each state took care of itself, unchecked by federal regulations. As a result, industries grew rapidly. But this "hands-off policy" created big cities that were ill-equipped to handle the problems of overpopulation. To make matters worse, by the end of the 1880s, city governments were littered with corrupt officials. Their power was based on exploiting the weak and poor, while befriending the rich and influential.

Imagine the shock of the immigrants as they arrived in the new land. Ignorant of America's ways and unable to speak its language, they sought refuge in the big cities along ethnic and national lines. Many ghettos were formed, each with different customs and speech patterns. These ghettos quickly turned into slums.

Rather than being a Garden of Eden, the big cities became centers of evil. Crime, vice, and violence were widespread. Illegal gambling went on in diners, candy stores, saloons, and pool halls. Lonely men and helpless women gave rise to the white slave trade, the then-popular name for prostitution. Opium dens operated everywhere. Robberies, beatings, rapes, murders, and "disappearances" were common events.

The newcomers had seen such conditions before. After all, many European cities had sinister underworld organizations running the same activities. Street gangs, secret societies, and violent hoodlums were what many immigrants were fleeing. In addition, the newcomers had no faith in politicians or law-enforcement officials. Experience had taught the poor that widespread crime existed because of political corruption, police protection, graft, and bribes.

To protect themselves, the slum-dwellers did what they had always done. They put their trust in people and groups they knew firsthand. The first wave of immigrants became too settled to move. So they set priorities for themselves. Most important was survival. That meant doing whatever had to be done to feed their families and protect their well-being. Next was learning the American way. The fastest, cheapest, and easiest method was to study the silent movies. And, finally, they worked for the day when they could escape the slums. Even if the first wave of immigrants failed, their children would make it. Ignorant of how to achieve their ends, the newcomers became easy victims of corrupt politicians and neighborhood thugs.

Every area had its gang wars battling for control of the streets. Often these groups disguised themselves as members of The Black Hand. Operated mostly by Italian and Sicilian gangsters, different individuals would band together and force slum-dwellers to pay them money for "protection." This extortion began by sending the intended victim a threatening note with the "signature" of a black hand. The fear of such a note made it easy for any gang to form a "black hand" organization. Although the slums were made up mostly of European immigrants, no one national or ethnic group had a monopoly on crime. The Chinese Tongs, for example, was a Cantonese gang specializing in drug peddling, gambling, and white slavery.

The most powerful groups soon became the infamous secret societies. They afforded their members the best protection and the most rewards. None was more successful than the Mafia. Modeled after its parent organization in Sicily, the American Mafia first intended to fight against government injustice and local tyranny. But soon its leaders became cruel and ruthless. They used violence to gain profit for themselves rather than to help the underprivileged. To join the evil brotherhood, you first had to be a native-born Sicilian. Second was to swear undying allegiance to the boss. Third was to consider an attack on any *Mafioso* as a personal attack that needed avenging no matter what the price or danger. Fourth was the promise never to deal with police or government authorities. And fifth was the vow of silence, *omerta,* pledging never to betray the Mafia. The penalty for breaking this pledge was death.

Uncertain just what would appeal to such a varied audience in the slum theaters, the pioneer film-makers experimented with different types of stories. The plan, still practiced today, was to find a popular subject and then repeat it over and over again. Sensational stories about crime and violence proved to be profitable. In *Revenge* (1904), a policeman's abuse of his power results in the death of a mother and her daughter. In *The Black Hand* (1906), Italian gangsters are shown terrorizing their fellow immigrants. In *The Fatal Hour* (1908), Chinese hoodlums try to force helpless young women into prostitution.

Crime movies proved popular not only because they seemed realistic, but also because they often took the side of the criminals. Poverty and despair, not the evilness in people, were shown as the main reasons for crime. *The Ex-Convict* and *The Eviction* (both made in 1905) were typical. In the former, an ex-convict cannot find work so he can feed his starving wife and get medical aid for his sick child. He is thus forced to return to a life of crime. In the latter film, a discouraged husband finds comfort only in alcoholism. His drinking results in his family being turned out into the streets and almost destroyed.

Such movies, big-city slums, and the rising crime rate in America soon became a national scandal. Many reformers, searching for an easy answer to a difficult problem, made movies the scapegoat for the nation's evils. The do-gooders argued that the slum theaters had replaced the home, schools, and religious institutions as the sources of American values. If the traditional groups could regain control of the country's morals, the reformers reasoned, then big-city evils could be curbed. The plan, therefore, was to control the content of moving pictures. As a result, censorship boards and laws sprang up everywhere in the early 1900s.

Although ineffective, such actions worried the film-makers. By 1910, close to 25 million people were going to the movies each week. Over the next decade, the figures would reach 40 million. Movies were fast becoming big business. And the film-makers wanted to protect their interests. To do that, they needed to be accepted by the "right people." So they moved the films out of the slum theaters and into more respectable buildings and areas. Feature films were introduced. A star system was created.

Such sweeping changes affected the movie gangster. The biggest step was to present his lifestyle in more detail. The 1912 movie *The Musketeers of Pig Alley* was the most authentic. Directed by D. W. Griffith, it focused on crime in the slums. The film's advertising declared, "Much is printed from time to time in the newspapers on the workings of gangsters, but the public gains but a vague idea of the actual facts. Hence this picture production, which does not run very strong as to plot, is simply intended to show vividly the doings of the gangster type of people."

Besides raising the art of moving pictures, *The Musketeers* . . . outlined how street gangs worked. Griffith showed them limiting their crime and violence to a few city blocks at a time. Their money was made from petty robberies and extortion. The movie made clear that ghetto crime was still a small-time operation.

The following year authentic crime stories about white slavery proved even more popular at the box office. The trend began with *Traffic in Souls*. Once again, studio advertising revealed how sex and crime could lure audiences to the theaters: "TRAFFIC IN SOULS—The sensational motion picture dramatization based on the Rockefeller White Slavery Report and on the investigation of the Vice Trust by District Attorney Whitman—A $200,000 spectacle [in fact, the film cost less than $6,000 to make] in 700 scenes with 800 players, showing the traps cunningly laid for young girls by vice agents—Don't miss the most thrilling scene ever staged, the smashing of the vice trust." *Traffic in Souls* made clear in early film history that sex and crime were two key factors in the economic success of a movie.

The first great feature film to link organized crime and social injustice was Griffith's *Intolerance* (1916). In this epic

D.W. Griffith's The Musketeers of Pig Alley *(1912) was the first significant gangster film. It concerned a young wife (Lillian Gish) being bothered by a neighborhood gangster (Elmer Booth).*

The first great feature film about gangsters was Griffith's Intolerance (1916). In the modern story, later released separately as The Mother and the Law, three young people migrate to the big city. Above: The Boy (Robert Harron) and The Friendless One (Miriam Cooper) are drawn into the gangster's world by The Musketeer of the Slums (Walter Long) in the center. Right: The Dear One (Mae Marsh) finds herself alone in the slums. The message throughout the film was that poor people are left with little dignity and protection.

movie about injustice through the ages, the great director examined four different historical periods and showed their similarities. The modern story stressed how a big city corrupted country hicks as well as immigrants.

In addition to revolutionizing film editing, set construction, and screen acting, *Intolerance* cemented many characteristics of future gangster movies. Its semidocumentary style is still impressive today. Memorable scenes of a labor strike ruthlessly broken by violence and bloodshed; a reform group operated by self-righteous, intolerant women; a desperate boy forced by poverty into a life of crime; a defenseless mother robbed of her baby; and a friendless girl drawn into vice were convincing proof that the greatest crimes were not always those performed by the poor. Griffith's views on the plight of the slum-made gangster made *Intolerance* an unforgettable motion picture.

If not for World War I and its aftereffects, the movie gangster might have lost his popularity. By 1917 a small band of film tycoons, using questionable methods, had begun to take over the entire American film industry. Through costly mergers and investments, these aggressive men set up "vertical" organizations that controlled production, distribution, and exhibition. World War I added to their power by destroying their foreign competition. Thus, Hollywood became the film capital of the world. Burdened by tremendous expenses, the new film tycoons tried to avoid any controversy that might reduce box-office profits. Films about gangsters were on their way out.

Then came one of American's most disastrous mistakes. Entry into World War I had left the federal government sympathetic to the demands of small but well-organized reform groups. One such organization was the Prohibition Party. For over forty years the group had tried in vain to have a constitutional amendment passed forbidding the sale of alcohol. Finally, in the high-minded spirit of 1917, Congress agreed to outlaw alcoholic sales to servicemen. Later that same year Congress passed the Eighteenth Amendment, which outlawed the sale of liquor after midnight of January 16, 1920. Within thirteen months, thirty-six well-intentioned, but misguided, states made the Volstead Prohibition Act the law of the land.

It was the signal for organized crime to move out of its neighborhoods and become big business. Looking back at the times we can see why. First is the knowledge that organized crime thrives by giving the public what the people want, but aren't legally allowed to have. Gambling, dope, and prostitution are prime examples. And as of January 16, 1920, the illegal sale of liquor opened up a rich new industry for mobsters.

To satisfy the nation's great thirst, large-scale criminal organizations were needed. Gangster movies over the next fifty years would reconstruct the explosive gang wars waged for control of the bootlegging market. Led by second-generation Americans, mostly Sicilians, Jews, and Irishmen, the Prohibition gangs at first were pictured as rugged individualists. Almost every household knew through their daily newspapers of legendary figures such as Al Capone, Charles "Lucky" Luciano, Arnold Rothstein, Jack "Legs" Diamond, Meyer Lansky, Dutch Schultz, Louis "Lepke" Buchalter, and Eugene Moran. Many would eventually be the subjects of films. Authors like F. Scott Fitzgerald, Damon Runyon, Raymond Chandler, and Dashiell Hammett would immortalize their types in fiction.

A second reason that organized crime grew so big during this era was the government's neglect of working class people. Poverty, slums, and corruption were ignored. Add to that the mass unemployment faced by World War I veterans and you can sense the anger brewing in America. The nation grew more restless and bitter with each passing year. The discontented learned a lesson never intended by those who shaped the values of the American Dream. That warped lesson was that survival and respect depended not on issues of right or wrong, but on whether you were smart or stupid. Thus the violence bred in the slums spread across the entire nation.

Still another reason for the rise of organized crime was the public's attitude toward Prohibition. They didn't like it and had no intention of helping enforce the foolish law. Furthermore, World War I had left many Americans disillusioned. They felt the war might have been for nothing. Even worse, the public soon discovered that their government was corrupt. "The Harding administration was responsible in two short years," wrote one historian, "for more concentrated robbery and rascality than any other in the whole history of the federal government." Small wonder then that Americans had contempt for the law. They moved into an era that prized money, material possessions, recklessness, a disregard for traditional values, and a passion for excitement. Such a climate was ideal for organized crime.

The feeling that lawbreaking was fashionable repopularized the Hollywood gangster. The image of the hard-boiled criminal of the pre-war days was revised for the early twenties. Film after film pictured him as the suave host to the "smart set." He ran speakeasies, gambling rooms, and roadhouses. Rather than being a threat to society, he was a clever man who made his living by giving the public what it wanted. His fancy clothes, influential friends, and beautiful women turned him into an attractive figure.

Melodramatic movies featuring gangsters, bootleggers, racketeers, and hijackers rarely took a serious look at organized crime. *The Penalty* (1920) focused on a man whose legs are needlessly amputated, and as a result, he revenges himself on society by becoming the head of San Francisco's underworld. Only Lon Chaney's striking acting as the hopeless cripple made the incredible story a box-office hit. *Heroes of the Street* (1922) also played on the revenge theme. A policeman's son, helped by a brave chorus girl, captures his father's killer and breaks up a gang of blackmailers. *Rags to Riches* (1922) is about a rich kid running away from home to join a gang of criminals and have some excitement. Only clever policework prevents him from destroying his life.

Reformers were shocked and angered by Hollywood's films. Just as disturbing was the film community's moral standards. Hardly a week passed without newspapers and fan magazines painting Hollywood as the new Sodom and Gomorrah. Stories about movie people's lives, which focused on dope addiction, sexual orgies, wild drinking parties, illegal gambling, sensational divorces, homosexuality, prostitution, suicides, and murders, scandalized people across the country.

By 1922, the reformers were on the verge of doing to films what they had done to the alcohol industry. No less than thirty-six different states had censorship bills ready to be voted into law. The film community panicked. Such laws would destroy the industry's ever-growing profits. To protect themselves, the movie tycoons hired Will H. Hays to be their spokesman. Then postmaster general of the United States and an elder in the Presbyterian church, Hays had the right "moral" credentials. Based upon his promise to reform the movie industry from within, the censors gave Hollywood a second chance.

At first, Hays made little progress. In fact, gangster films became more realistic as the nation began to take a more sober look at organized crime. Newspaper accounts of the bloody Mafia civil wars in New York, Al Capone's violent empire in Chicago, and the infamous Cleveland syndicate dramatized the threat that gangsters posed for the entire country. Thus, films like *Chicago* (1925) and *The Street of Forgotten Men* (1927) exposed how the cruel city life encouraged crime and racketeering.

In an attempt to make crime less attractive to audiences, Hays, in June 1927, persuaded the movie tycoons to adopt an ethical production policy. This first set of systematic rules for

In the 1920s crime, drinking, and sex were fashionable. In Warner Brothers' Rags to Riches (1922), a young playboy (Wesley Barry) joins a gang to get some excitement. His plan backfires when the hoodlums try to kidnap him and ask his family for a large ransom. Niles Welch, masquerading as a gangster is, in fact, a secret service agent.

Josef von Sternberg's Underworld *was the last important silent gangster film. It concerned a tough gangster (George Bancroft) whose life of crime led him to his fateful, violent death.*

moral behavior in American movies was known as "Don'ts and Be Carefuls." The restrictions started with how crimes against the law were to be treated. Sympathy could not be with the criminals. Plots or characters should not inspire antisocial acts. Criminal methods or murder techniques had to be quickly shown so as not to teach young people new methods of crime. The illegal drug trade could not be made exciting so as to make audiences curious about its stimulating experiences. And the use of alcohol in American life was allowed only when necessary for plot or character development.

Two months later, the silent film industry circulated the last important gangster movie, *Underworld*. Written by Ben Hecht, an ex-reporter turned novelist, playwright, and screenwriter, the film was a nostalgic look at Chicago crime. Mobster Bull Weed (George Bancroft) lived only for his girl friend Feathers (Evelyn Brent). When Bull is sent to jail and she falls in love with his best friend (Clive Brooks), the gangster breaks out, seeking revenge. But he discovers that love cannot be denied and his own strong code of honor forces him to forgive them and Bull dies in a shoot-out with the police. Directed by Josef von Sternberg, the romantic film visually captured a criminal world unto itself. Although the public loved Sternberg's photographic sentiment, Hecht hated the finished product and wired the director, "You poor ham; take my name off the film."

While *Underworld* was playing in movie theaters, Warner Brothers' studio released on October 6, 1927, the sensational sound film *The Jazz Singer*. That one film, more than any other, ended the silent film era.

Sound added a new "reality" to moving pictures. It increased the effect of what was seen on the screen. And the more real the movies became, the more popular was the gangster movie. Audiences, now excited about sound movies, thrilled to the sounds of the gangster's world: police sirens, machine-gun fire, screeching cars, tough-talking hoodlums, and wisecracking molls.

Below: Lewis Milestone's The Racket *(1928) explored the problems faced by honest policemen in fighting organized crime. It was a theme to become popular in many gangster movies. Thomas Meighan starred as the hard-boiled police captain. Opposite: the movie that summed up the first thirty years of gangster clichés was* Broadway *(1929). Robert Ellis (left) played the smooth bootlegger. Evelyn Brent was the young girl who witnesses a gangland killing. And Glenn Tryon (right) is the man suspected of a crime he didn't commit.*

As the public flocked to the "talkies," Hollywood studios increased their production of gangster movies. In 1928, for example, the first all-talking film was a Prohibition gangster tale, *The Docks of New York*. That same year also saw an increased realism in gangster behavior. Movies like *The Big City, Tenderloin, Chicago After Midnight,* and *The Dragnet* revealed just how vicious and widespread crime had become.

One of the most popular films in 1928 was *The Racket*. Produced by Howard Hughes and directed by Lewis Milestone, it showed how two rival bootleg kings battle for control of an area supervised by an honest police captain. Gangsters have fancy cars, a disregard for other people's rights, and a contempt for the law. The police captain's honesty is contrasted with an influential politician's corruption. Only after a cop is murdered is the police captain able to corner and kill the hard-boiled gang leader.

Inspired by the box-office profits of such films, the movie tycoons continued to ignore the Hays "formula." By the end of the twenties, gangster films like *Woman Trap, Alibi,* and *The Racketeer* (all in 1929) were mirroring the violence and crime in America's big cities. The public, shocked by Capone's massacre of a rival gang on St. Valentine's Day, could go to almost any local movie theater and see gangland methods, helpless policemen, and corrupt politicians on the screen.

Summing up how far the gangster film had come since its early slum theater days was *Broadway*. Based on a New York stageplay of the same title, the movie had all of the screen's gangster conventions: the typical nightclub environment, the rival gangster kings, the chorus girl in love with the decent guy, the innocent witness to a murder, the mistaken suspect, and the wisecracking, hard-hitting dialogue.

In October 1929, the stock market crashed, and the nation was set for organized crime, the Hollywood gangster, and the movie industry to enter a new era.

1929
HEADLINE HEROES
193-4

The popularity of gangster movies soared during the early thirties. Despite their brutal and tragic careers, the Hollywood gangsters emerged as smart guys. They climbed the ladder of success when everyone else seemed lost and hopeless.

Few movies, however, revealed the growing unrest in organized crime. As early as 1929, a nationwide pattern was developing. Clever and ambitious young mobsters, like Lucky Luciano, Frank Costello, and Vito Genovese, were rebelling against the older ganglords like Joe Masseria. The issues were clear. The elders clung to the traditional ways—killing anyone who bothered you, forming gangs along bloodlines, arguing every-man-for-himself. The new generation was more realistic —crime should be run like a business, gangs organized according to skills rather than national origins, killings carried out according to executive orders. Issues like these were pushing the underworld toward a bloody civil war.

In the meantime, MGM's *The Big House*, released in June 1930, struck out at prison life. Long considered the graduate school for gangsters, prisons rarely received screen attention. Directed by the imaginative George Hill, *The Big House* reversed that trend and set the basic pattern for future prison movies. Frances Marion's script followed the lives of three men sent to prison: Morgan (Chester Morris), a forger; Butch (Wallace Beery), a killer; and Kent Marlowe (Robert Montgomery), convicted of manslaughter because he killed someboy when he was driving a car while drunk. Notable scenes showed a new prisoner being processed, crowded prison conditions, the inmates' dislike of their meals, and the pathetic men mulling around prison yards. Best of all was the closing sequence in which army tanks had to be used to put down a prison uprising. *The Big House* also established Hill and Marion (married in real life) as artists able to blend sharp details into action stories.

The success of *The Big House* held little interest for MGM. It preferred making glamorous films rather than hard-hitting melodramas. Just the opposite was true for Warner Brothers. Now a major studio thanks to its leadership in the talkie revolution, Warners became identified with hard, fast, big-city movies.

An example of the studio's stress on social realism was *The Doorway to Hell* released late in 1930. George Rosener's screenplay sketched out what happened to an underworld bootlegging czar who tries to quit the rackets. More important than the thin plot was director Archie Mayo's handling of the characters and scenes. Gangsters clearly became identified with big-city life, tough talk, and dishonest traits. Despite their quick success, they were seen as doomed men whose search for material possessions and power ended tragically. Racketeering was shown as a vicious occupation, so powerful that the police appeared helpless. A particularly moving scene had the bootlegger visiting the slums where he was born, identifying his rat-infested house, and stating bitterly that his brother and sister died of typhoid. Equally effective is the moment when an honest police captain, knowing the courts can't convict the ganglord, allows him to escape, aware that rival gangsters will kill the ruthless hoodlum.

The Doorway to Hell, Warner Brothers' first major gangster film of the thirties, brought recognition to the studio's new young actor, James Cagney. Cast as the bootlegger's wise-cracking pal, Cagney's behavior in the film signaled the rise of a new star. As the years would prove, he was an ideal gangster. His tough guy, New York accent, his smug, dapper mannerisms, and his commanding personality all warned people not to be fooled by his charm. This urban slum kid was dangerous.

Yet Cagney's big break was still months away. For the moment, Darryl F. Zanuck, Warner's production head, speculated over new ways to cash in on the bloodbaths sweeping across the nation's streets. Up to that point, gangster movies had stressed romance mixed with violence and not hoodlums' pathetic lives. What if Warner's played down the romance and

Above: MGM's The Big House *started a trend for tough prison dramas. In this scene, Chester Morris (left) attempts to stop a prison riot. Robert Montgomery (third from left) has already warned the prison officials about the uprising. Right: Warner Brothers'* The Doorway to Hell *centered on the rise and fall of a beer baron. Billed as "the picture gangdom dared Hollywood to make," it brought recognition to a newcomer at the studio, James Cagney (right).*

upgraded its look at mob life itself? The answer came with the studio's December preview of a film based on W. R. Burnett's novel about the Chicago underworld, *Little Caesar*.

Under Mervyn LeRoy's tight, no-nonsense direction, *Little Caesar* made screen history. At first glance, the plot provided few new elements. Gangsters were still pictured as immigrants corrupted by the evil city, and rural values remained the hope for America. Hoodlums were tragic figures doomed by their misguided lust for clothes, cars, power, and money. No one denied that the characters once more symbolized the American Dream corrupted.

Little Caesar starred Edward G. Robinson as a Capone-like gangster whose lust for power destroys him. In this scene Robinson (standing) is given a testimonial dinner in honor of his new position in the mob.

But *Little Caesar* had many unique elements. It showed what prompted small-time hoodlums like Caesar Enrico Bandello to believe that crime gave them their only chance "to be somebody." With fast editing, LeRoy showed step-by-step Rico's rise and fall from gangland power. The film illustrated how headline mobsters inspired simpleminded hoodlums. It also illustrated how false the headlines were. Loyalty to one's family, friends, or heritage had tragic not noble results. Single-mindedness in getting ahead resulted not in fame or fortune but in betrayal and death. Once in the rackets, a hoodlum almost never escaped the gang alive. In addition to exposing the gangster's brutal life, *Little Caesar* contributed classic mob dialogue: "You can dish it out but you can't take it"; "Take him for a ride"; "big boy"; and "You know too much." And few viewers can forget Rico's final moment when, aware of who and what he is, the dying gangster, lying in the gutter, asks, "Mother of Mercy [some versions have "God"], is this the end of Rico?"

Crucial to the film's success, however, was Edward G. Robinson's performance as Rico. It was so memorable that the kind, gentle actor remained typecast as a cigar-smoking, tough-talking gangster throughout his long career. Asked often how he created the performance, Robinson explained in 1968, "It is far easier to do Ibsen, Shaw, or Shakespeare, than to create something from a one-dimensional character. For me, Rico in *Little Caesar* was a character in a Greek tragedy, a man who is reaching for the top and would sacrifice anything, even himself, to get it. I drew on those elements within myself to create the character."

The success of *Little Caesar* triggered off a whole cycle of gangster movies, the most famous being *The Public Enemy*. The screenplay, credited to reporters Kubec Glasmon and John Bright, summarizes a gangster's education from the gutter to the grave. Starting with the film's opening episode, set in 1909 to the tune of "I'm Forever Blowing Bubbles," director

William Wellman fashions a superb visual history of two street pals, Tom Powers and Matt Doyle. Poor slum kids, easily bored, they search for excitement in beer halls and poolrooms. Petty thefts win them friendships with neighborhood crooks who soon involve the tough kids in guns, robbery, and murder. Both Tom's widowed mother and older brother, Mike, are helpless to reform the misdirected young hoodlum. A famous episode has the two brothers arguing over Mike's patriotism and honesty. Tom thinks it stupid to enlist in World War I. As far as he's concerned, everyone should look out for himself. By 1921, Prohibition provides both Tom and Matt with a chance to move up the crime ladder. Their bootlegging careers bring them big bankrolls, fancy clothes, and flashy cars. Tom easily fools his confused mother with fake stories about his work. At the same time, he ridicules his brother's virtuous ways, labeling him a sucker. With gangland success also came fast women. Tom treats them as objects to be enjoyed and then

The Public Enemy was Cagney's fifth film and did not start out with him as the star. Edward Woods (left) had the key role of Tom Powers. Cagney played Matt Doyle. But three days into the shooting, everyone agreed that the roles were miscast and the parts were reversed. Jean Harlow, another movie beginner who was soon to become a famous star, played the rich girl out for a good time.

The gangster's "tragic flaw" is his love for a friend or a family member. The turning point in The Public Enemy *comes when Tom tries to avenge Matt's death.*

thrown away. The two friends, confident that they can't be stopped, begin terrorizing local shopkeepers into buying their gang's beer. The rival mob objects and ambushes the pair, killing Matt. Driven by vengeance, Tom singlehandedly raids the rival gang's headquarters and is seriously wounded in the shootout. Then, in one of film history's most unforgettable endings, the rival gang telephones Tom's mother, saying they're bringing her son home from the hospital. Happy, she goes upstairs to make his bed, while the brother goes to the door, opens it, and sees Tom's corpse, wrapped up like a mummy, fall dead on the floor.

The Public Enemy, released in April 1931, became the yardstick to measure all future gangster films by. Beautifully constructed and richly detailed, it became the model for crime stories right up to the present day. Ambitious gangsters were the key figures. Their antisocial attitudes reflected their tough, immigrant, slum background. Their success was equated with power and luxuries. Friends, family, and women presented opposite values that were ridiculed. Women, in particular, got categorized as mothers, mistresses, sisters, or ladies. Yet the gangster's love for a friend or relative resulted in his eventual violent death.

Still the most remarkable feature of *The Public Enemy* is Cagney as the unrepentant Tom Powers. Here was a swaggering gangster who symbolized the era's cynicism. He distrusted the rich, scorned traditional values, and preoccupied himself with getting ahead. Add to this the ex-vaudevillian's quick, graceful movements, an infectious grin, and a breathy, crisp speech and you begin to understand his dazzling appeal. Cagney's best moments in the film also bring out his dark humor. One scene has him sadistically shoving a grapefruit in Mae Clarke's face. Another episode has him shooting a horse responsible for killing his idolized boss. Consequently, *The Public Enemy* had the effect of typecasting Cagney just as *Little Caesar* had typecast Robinson.

Popular gangster films did more than make stars out of their leading players. Often scripted with the sound revolution in mind, they specialized in sharp, biting dialogue. This, in turn, affected the editing techniques, forcing the action to move quickly and tightly. Speed, excitement, the up-to-date tone, realistic characters and events soon advanced the art of the new talking films. Audiences, understandably, clamored for more gangster films along the Robinson-Cagney lines. Hollywood greedily obliged. Before the year was out, over fifty-one gangster films had been produced and distributed throughout the land.

Most of these films were poor imitations. MGM's *The Secret Six* was the exception. Once again, teaming director George Hill, screenwriter Frances Marion, and actor Wallace Beery proved a winning combination. The fast-moving story followed the efforts of crusading citizens set on wiping out organized crime in their city. To keep their identities secret, they wear masks when examining or questioning witnesses. The major villains are a corrupt criminal attorney (Lewis Stone) and his murderous gangster friend Scorpio (Beery).

The Secret Six added a new direction to the gangster cycle in 1931. It focused attention on the crusaders instead of the criminals. Here we see Clark Gable (hands behind his back) being threatened by Wallace Beery (center) while Jean Harlow watches.

Two reporters (Clark Gable and John Mack Brown) hired to gather evidence get sidetracked momentarily by Scorpio's girl friend (Jean Harlow). But when she falls for Brown, Scorpio has him killed and brings about his own downfall. Cornered in the end by the police, Scorpio murders his attorney before being captured, and thus provides the evidence necessary for the state to execute him.

There may have been better gangster films than *The Secret Six,* but none more successfully pointed the formula in new directions. The Hill-Marion techniques downplayed romantic elements. Working closely with lighting expert Harold Wenstrom, they pictured bootlegging as a slimy, grubby operation that took place in crowded basements. Everyday sounds of the city replaced the standard musical effects. Decades later, television adopted the idea of a morally indignant group with special police powers to destroy bootlegging operations in the highly successful TV series, *The Untouchables.* Another trend-setting device had gangster types switching to good guy roles. Clark Gable, known up to 1931 for playing tough hoods, made the move to hero parts in *The Secret Six* and headed for stardom. Oddly enough, a national screen magazine felt it necessary that year to warn its readers that Gable was not a typical gangster type.

Seen from today's perspective, this famous gangster cycle based on newspaper headlines missed the real story of the day. Big time bootleggers had known by the time *The Doorway to Hell* was released that Prohibition was doomed. Since they had no intention of going "legit," the smart mobsters began searching for new money-making operations. Some like Louis "Lepke" Buchalter specialized in labor and industry extortion. Dutch Schultz struck it big in restaurant "protection." Others tried narcotics. Most found gambling a profitable market.

With the underworld's shift to new territories came the long expected, bloody civil war. Ironically, films like *Little Caesar* and *The Public Enemy* supported the stand taken by the modern gangsters that individualism was bad business. The new money-making ventures required the security-minded gangsters to rid themselves of types like Rico and Scorpio. To this end Lucky Luciano met with other important ganglords in a series of secret meetings between 1928 and early 1931. Their decisions dramatically changed the underworld. First, plans were made to eliminate the old-time gangsters. Next they proposed to form a cartel, in this case a national syndicate to regulate organized crime. The syndicate, run by a board of directors, would settle arguments between gangs, state policy, and negotiate controversial deals. Big-city bosses benefited by teaming their individual gangs with other independent organizations on a national scale. They gained protection for their territory. They gained a wider market for their goods. Most important, the syndicate promised security.

After months of careful planning, the Luciano group made its move on September 11, 1931. Remembered as the "night of the Sicilian Vespers," close to forty Mafia members were murdered over a two-day period. So skillful were the executions that years passed before anyone connected the various deaths to a mass-murder operation.

While the underworld profited from the new wave of violence, Hollywood did not. Criticism against the film capital reached new heights. Leading the attack were prominent religious groups. Citing the gangster cycle as their prime example, they charged the movie industry with undermining America's values. Weekend audiences, 90 percent of which were children, made glamorized gangsters their heroes. Films about political corruption, police brutality, adultery, premarital sex, vulgarity, and disrespect for parents glorified "sin." The church leaders ridiculed movies like *Little Caesar* and *The Public Enemy* with their tacked-on prologues and epilogues about the evils of crime. The reformers didn't buy the argument that the violent gangsters' death showed "crime didn't pay."

Multimillionaire Howard Hughes unwittingly helped the crusaders' cause. Early in 1931, he had set out to exploit the popularity of the gangster cycle. Hughes convinced Ben Hecht to write a screenplay (based on a book by Armitage Trail) about a modern-day Borgia family living in Chicago. The main role, a Caesar Borgia character, was modeled after Alphonse "Scarface" Capone. Then director Howard Hawks took over. Beginning that spring, he assembled an unknown cast, including Paul Muni, George Raft, and Boris Karloff. For several months the team filmed a story that followed many of the by-now standardized conventions used in *Little Caesar* and *The Public Enemy:* gang rivalries, ambitious hoods, conflicting values.

What made *Scarface* so extraordinary was Hawks' visual ingenuity. One of his favorite thematic devices was to have the

Many film critics consider Howard Hughes' production Scarface *the best of the thirties gangster films. Paul Muni played the obsessed Tony Camonte doomed to a savage death.*

camera isolate the letter X anytime a murder occurred. When Karloff, for example, is killed during a bowling match, we see a closeup of his bowling scoresheet: a strike. Raft dies in an apartment marked with the Roman numeral X. Another thematic device pictured a flashing window sign, "The World is Yours . . . Cook's Tours." It symbolized the gangster's false dreams. These devices coupled with sensational shoot-outs and car wrecks made *Scarface* the most authentic gangster film of the cycle.

Reformers were enraged by the film's authenticity and documentary style. First came attacks from the Hays Office. Demands were made to tone down the hard-bitten dialogue and twisted humor. Then came orders to cut specific shots, add an additional scene denouncing organized crime, change the ending so that Scarface is executed by the state instead of shot down in the street, and provide a new title, "Shame of the Nation." A year passed between the end of the shooting and the film's actual release to the public in mid-1932. Even then, the censorship battle continued. State censorship boards along with major cities banned the movie. Not until Hughes went to court did *Scarface* get widely seen.

Fueling the censorship fires was Paul Muni's magnificent performance as the brutal Tony Camonte. Made up with an ugly gash across his face, he growled, laughed, killed, and, in the end, showed just how cowardly gangsters could become. Muni provided audiences with one of the screen's most complex mobster images. Rave reviews gave him the same chance for stardom that *Little Caesar* and *The Public Enemy* had given Robinson and Cagney. But Muni was different. He never wanted the "slavery of stardom." As a result, the great character actor refused to play the same role twice.

Muni's decision mattered little by 1933. Hollywood was again in a state of panic. Box-office figures had fallen to sixty million customers a week, down thirty million since 1930. Films like *Scarface* had resulted in well-organized campaigns to boycott "offensive" movies. In addition, public opinion had changed. The kidnapping and murder of Charles Lindbergh's baby the previous year had soured audiences on gangster movies. The fact that so many of them were quickly made imitations also helped kill their appeal. Furthermore, Congress voted in the Twenty-first Amendment, which ended Prohibition on December 5, 1933. Faced with possible collapse, the motion-picture industry gave up and the censors took charge.

A motion-picture production code the Hays Office had proposed back in 1930 when the great gangster cycle first began was now strictly enforced. Starting in June 1934, Hollywood changed its approach to crime films with specific regulations:

"(I) Crime Against the Law. These shall never be presented in such a way as to show sympathy with the crime as against law and justice or to inspire others with a desire for imitation.

(1) *Murder*
   (a) The technique of murder must be presented in a way that will not inspire imitation.
   (b) Brutal killings are not to be presented in detail.
   (c) Revenge in modern times shall not be justified.

(2) *Methods of crime should not be explicitly presented.*
   (a) Theft, robbery, safecracking, and dynamiting of trains, mines, buildings, etc., should not be detailed in method.
   (b) Arson must be subject to the same safeguards.
   (c) The use of firearms should be restricted to essentials.
   (d) Methods of smuggling should not be presented."

The code worked, but in a way never guessed by the censors. Hollywood came up with a new get-rich idea that featured violence.

1935
SWITCH
1939

J. Edgar Hoover may seem an unlikely person to credit with starting a new gangster film cycle in 1935. As director of the Federal Bureau of Investigation he naturally hated movies that glamorized gangsters. Yet his actions in the thirties triggered a return to fast-action crime films.

Ever since taking over the Bureau in 1924, Hoover fought to improve the agency's image. That was no easy job. His agents couldn't carry guns or make arrests. Besides, organized crime was too large for his undermanned squads to fight. Then came the public uproar over the Lindbergh case, and Congress passed in 1932 a law making kidnapping a federal crime. This gave the federal agents power to act effectively in their war against gangsters. Hoover seized the moment to publicize how the Bureau was society's major safeguard against crime. It wasn't true, particularly since the Treasury Department had been the major force in sending Al Capone to jail in 1931 for tax evasion. But Hoover devised a brilliant scheme. Through his contacts in the mass media, he published a Public Enemy list of the nation's "most desperate" criminals. The list came out at the time the FBI was set to capture these gangsters. Hoover's brilliance lay in turning small-time, Midwestern hoodlums like Alvin "Old Creepy" Karpis, "Pretty Boy" Floyd, Bonnie Parker, Clyde Barrow, "Ma" Barker, "Machine Gun" Kelly, and John Dillinger into national problems. Unable to fight organized crime's giant army, Hoover went after smaller hoods and made it seem big stuff.

"Machine Gun" Kelly illustrates the Public Enemy game the FBI played. Kelly was a small-time bootlegger who often bragged "no copper would ever take me alive." His showoff ways fooled few people. They knew he was stupid, easy-going, and drank too much. His image changed, however, when he married Cleo Shannon. She wanted a headline gangster for a husband. So Cleo bought him a machine gun, nagged George into robbing some banks, and insisted that he kidnap a millionaire oilman. Kelly's fear and incompetence almost wrecked the ranson arrangements. Soon after the victim's release, a Tennessee policeman burst into Kelly's hideout and captured the meek outlaw. Hoover, however, made sure that Americans believed this "public menace" was pursued and captured by the FBI. Newspapers reported the terrified gangster as yelling, "Don't shoot G-Men!"

Warner Brothers decided to cash in on Hoover's commitment to improving the public image of the FBI. They saw it as a way around the studio's censorship battles over gangster films. If you made the crusading lawman the hero, you could still emphasize fast-paced, violent action.

In 1935, the studio experimented with William Keighley's *G-Men*. The sly melodrama dealt with a slum kid who is sent to law school by a friendly gangster. When a college friend is later killed trying to arrest a hoodlum, the young lawyer joins the FBI, seeking revenge for the murder. Using his former underworld contacts, he discovers his benefactor's role in the crime and kills him in a shoot-out. He then decides to quit the Bureau but changes his mind when another gang kidnaps his girl friend. He rescues her and wins the Department's respect.

By using Cagney as the reformed crusader, Warner Brothers successfully merged the old and new gangster formulas. The public saw their popular star doing what he had always done, only now on the side of justice. Furthermore, censors couldn't complain. More important, gangster films had new ingredients. Old-time villains with slum backgrounds were replaced by new front-page mobsters, native-born, and residing in rural areas. Instead of the standard bootlegging stories, audiences got bank robbers, kidnappings, and interstate manhunts.

The Petrified Forest directed by Archie Mayo in 1936 gave Warners' its next major gangster film. Though mainly a photographed stageplay, its theme of brute force versus intellectualism proved popular with audiences. The story dealt with a mixed group of people held captive in an isolated

The Petrified Forest *turned Robert Sherwood's Broadway hit into a popular gangster film. Leslie Howard (left) and Bette Davis played the hopeless lovers kept at bay by the merciless Humphrey Bogart. Dick Foran (center) was the lady's jealous boyfriend.*

Above: Edward G. Robinson played a crusading cop who destroys Humphrey Bogart's underworld mob in Bullets or Ballots. *Below:* G-Men *had Cagney switching sides and becoming an FBI agent to revenge a friend's death. Here he faces Edward Pawley and Barton MacLane.*

service station by the vicious Duke Mantee and his gang escaping from the law. Despite the talky script, the dialogue produced some memorable observations about gangsters. Upon meeting Mantee, the hero (Leslie Howard), a penniless intellectual with a death wish, raises his glass and declares, "You're the last great apostle of rugged individualism." Another character argues that Mantee isn't a gangster. "Gangsters are foreigners, he's an American." Elsewhere Mantee himself summarizes a gangster's story, "I've spent most of my time since I grew up in jail . . . and it looks like I'll spend the rest of my life dead."

Still the best part of *The Petrified Forest* is Humphrey Bogart as the brutal Mantee. Tough, cynical, menacing, the rugged actor offered a sharp contrast to the by-now-familiar swaggering, optimistic screen gangsters. Bogart moved slowly about the set, wearing a two-day beard, his body visibly slumped over suggesting an apelike mentality that threatened mankind. The Mantee role (originally slated for Edward G. Robinson but gotten for Bogart by Leslie Howard) saved Bogart's film career. Having done ten bad movies prior to *The Petrified Forest*, he seemed unsuited for Hollywood. This film proved to be the turning point. Bogart remained typecast over the next few years as a sneering, heartless gangster who dies in the end and became a fixed member of Warner's immortal murderer's row, which includes James Cagney, Paul Muni, Edward G. Robinson, and George Raft.

The same year saw Robinson switch to the right side of the law in *Bullets or Ballots*. Based loosely on Manhattan detective Johnny Broderick's exploits, Seton I. Miller's screenplay dealt with the special powers granted crusading policemen. William Keighley's taut direction deglamorized racket life and made crime-busters the heroic figures. Robinson played a tough cop who fakes his dismissal in order to join Bogart's mob and then destroy it. The role appealed to Robinson, who explained in an interview, "It was a hard part—I had to play it differently from those gangster roles, play it down, make it quieter... Even so, in that scene where I had to convince the audience as well as the gang that I was turning racketeer, I could see a trace of Little Caesar again." Bogart's role, on the other hand, played both on his Mantee image and the real-life Dutch Schultz. The actor now became typecast as an unrepentant, calculating, and double-crossing mobster.

This cycle of gangster films brought back Hollywood's attacks on the social conditions that breed criminals. Signaling the return was director William Wyler's 1937 screen adaptation of Sidney Kingsley's Broadway hit *Dead End*. The United Artists film pictured the conflicting lifestyles in New York City's East River district, where luxury and poverty existed side by side. Six young boys, headed for trouble, meet the notorious "Baby Face" Martin (Bogart), who revisits the old neighborhood to see his mother (Marjorie Main) and take up with his old girl friend (Claire Trevor). A poor but talented architect (Joel McCrea) and a sister of one of the boys (Sylvia Sidney) join forces to oppose the gangster's influence on the Dead End kids. Although forced by the Motion Picture Code to downplay violence and eliminate vulgarity, screenwriter Lillian Hellman successfully captured the play's powerful message about poverty, ignorance, and neglect. One unforgettable scene had the gangster's mother slapping him in the face and growling, "You dog, you dirty yellow dog, you! You ain't no son of mine!" His bitter response, "I killed a guy for looking at me the way you are now." Another famous exchange occurs when the mobster discovers that his old girl friend is a prostitute. Horrified he barks, "Why didn't you starve?" Her quick reply is, "Why didn't you?" Most popular with audiences of the day was the realistic acting of the Dead End kids themselves. Brought to Hollywood from their roles in the original stageplay, the youngsters went on to become movie fixtures for the next two decades.

Angels With Dirty Faces (1938) further advanced the

argument that criminals are made not born. The cliché-ridden story of two boyhood chums—one a gangster (Cagney) and the other a priest (Pat O'Brien)—took a hard look at rat-infested tenements, hoodlum influence on neighborhood slum kids, and ineffectual settlement-house programs. At one point, Father Connolly grudgingly admits to Rocky Sullivan, "Whatever I teach them, you show me up. You show them the easiest way." Admitting that crime appears profitable and gangster behavior seems heroic, the dedicated priest pleads with the soon-to-be executed gangster to destroy the Dead End kids' worship of Rocky. "You've been a hero to them in life, and if you go to the chair without a quiver, you'll be a hero to them in death. I want them to despise your memory. They've got to be ashamed of you." The film's climax has the gangster screaming that he doesn't want to die, but Michael Curtiz directs the

In Angels With Dirty Faces, *one of the Dead End kids reads about Cagney's death.*

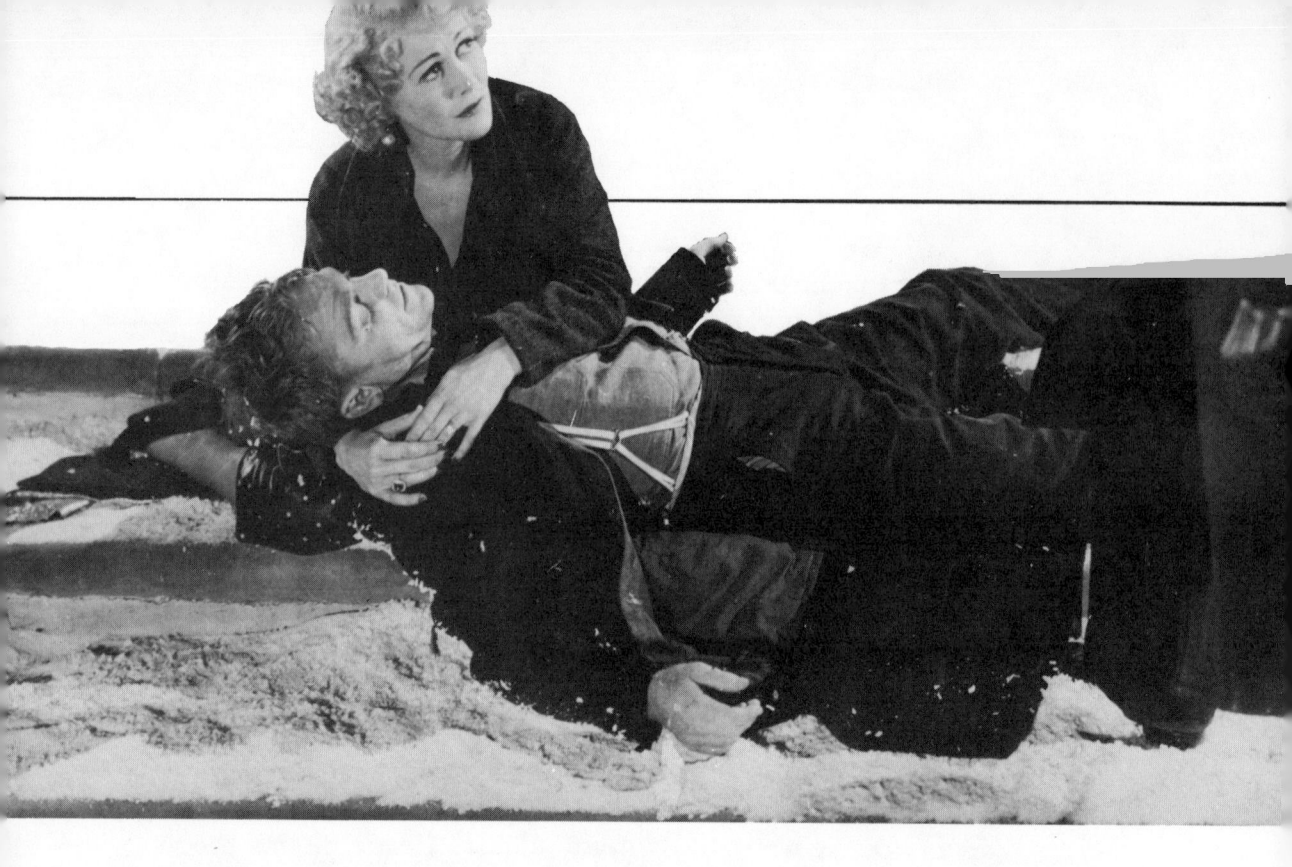

Above: in this famous death scene from The Roaring Twenties, a policeman asks Gladys George what the victim's business was, and she replies, "He used to be a big shot!" *Below:* newspaper comic strip heroes were popular in movie serials. Mystery was a key ingredient. Either the villain or the hero kept their identities secret until the last exciting chapter. Typical is the masked scorpion using George Pembroke as a hostage to escape from Tom Tyler in *Republic's* The Adventures of Captain Marvel.

scene with such subtlety that no one ever knows whether Rocky died a coward or hero. Aided considerably by performers like Cagney, O'Brien, the Dead End kids, Bogart, and Ann Sheridan, *Angels With Dirty Faces* emerged as the best gangster film of the late thirties.

The Golden Age of gangster films faded by the end of the decade. One reason was that producers just burnt out the formula. No matter how hard-boiled Bogart might be in a film like *Racket Busters* (1938), you knew he was a loser. The same predictability hurt Raoul Walsh's *The Roaring Twenties* (1939). Audiences were bored by the old familiar Prohibition stories. Not even humorous attempts like *A Slight Case of Murder* (1938), which turned Robinson's Little Caesar role into broad comedy, revived sagging box-office profits. Another reason the public lost interest was the tie existing between the gangster movies and "headline news." By 1938, the famous public enemies were dead or behind bars. Tough-minded crime-busters like Thomas E. Dewey had finished their sensational investigations and a false sense of confidence swept the nation. Gangsters no longer seemed a threat to society. The danger now came from foreign agents, and studios like Warner Brothers began shifting the crime conventions to espionage films like *Confessions of a Nazi Spy* (1939).

About the only formula profiting from gangster types in the late thirties was the serial. Here again newspapers provided the inspiration. Many comic strip heroes such as Dick Tracy, Captain Marvel, and Superman fitted ideally into the weekly chapter format. The standard plot featured a dangerous gang pitted against the forces of justice. Typical was Republic's *Dick Tracy Returns* (1938) in which the master lawman joins the ranks of federal agents through fifteen episodes to destroy the notorious Pa Stark gang.

Hollywood thus had two choices in 1939: Either forget about gangster films or find another way to make use of the once popular violent material.

19-40
A NEW TRADITION
19-49

America learned shocking facts about war and organized crime in the forties. It discovered that President Roosevelt's attack on big-city bosses with their corrupt and graft-ridden administrations fostered the growth of the syndicate. Gangsters fleeing the "big heat" in New York, Pennsylvania, Illinois, Ohio, and Massachusetts, set up new crime operations in Florida, Arizona, and California. Until early 1940, the public believed that gangbusters like Hoover and Dewey had broken the back of organized crime. Major mobsters like Luciano were in jail, while others were being deported monthly.

Then came the sensational probe by assistant district attorney Burton Turkus into Brooklyn crime. A two-bit murderer named Abe "Kid Twist" Reles confessed he belonged to an elite group that killed-by-contract. Victims were selected by gangs across the country and then okayed by national criminals like Lepke, Benjamin "Bugsy" Siegel, and Albert Anastasia. As the case against "Murder Inc." unfolded, Turkus revealed the vast criminal network covering the nation, corrupting government on all levels, state and federal law-enforcement bodies, and labor and management groups. The syndicate's power thrived on the revelations. Since Murder Inc. included old-fashioned killers like Lepke, their conviction and execution eliminated outmoded gangsters. The gangland killing of the "canary" Reles, who was thrown out of a heavily guarded police hotel window, let the public know that no one was safe when the syndicate was after you. The fact that Siegel and Anastasia escaped criminal prosecution proved the syndicate's power.

The forties also saw a major change in gangster films. Crimes became more terrifying, the characters more dishonest and double-dealing. Announcing the end of the old formulas in 1941 was director Raoul Walsh's *High Sierra*.

Scripted by John Huston and W. R. Burnett, the nostalgic plot was Hollywood's way of saying goodbye to a folk hero of the depression. Sprung from jail by a fatally ill gangland pal,

High Sierra *lionized the Depression gangster. Bogart portrayed the tragic Roy "Mad Dog" Earle forced to work with young twerps like Arthur Kennedy and Alan Curtis (kneeling). Ida Lupino turned in a superb performance as the gun moll, who sympathizes with Earle's predicament.*

Roy "Mad Dog" Earle discovers that organized crime as he knew it is no more. His friend tells him that screwballs have taken over: "Young twerps, soda jerkers and jitterbugs.... Yep, all the A-1 guys are gone. Dead—or in Alcatraz...." Committed to doing the ill-fated bank robbery, Earle finds himself confused and alone in the modern criminal setting. "Sometimes," he observes, "I feel I don't know what it's all about any more." The robbery itself reveals that the gangster's new associates are inexperienced, cowardly, and disloyal. Accepting his tragic destiny, the Dillinger-like Earle chooses to make his last stand high in the mountains, symbolic of his isolation from the world around him.

High Sierra not only put aside old formulas, but also ended Bogart's days as a "minor" gangster figure next to Cagney and Robinson. Their refusal to play the Earle role—they didn't want a part George Raft had turned down—provided Bogart with one of his best acting jobs. Even more significant, *High Sierra* promoted him to star status.

Later that same year Bogart ushered in a new era for gangster movies with *The Maltese Falcon*. Cast as the cynical, tough private eye Sam Spade, he turned Warner Brothers' third version of the Dashiell Hammett novel into a film masterpiece. The story, brilliantly scripted and filmed by John Huston in his directorial debut, studied what happens when a San Francisco detective agrees to help a beautiful but murderous lady gain possession of a legendary jeweled statuette. Cinematographer Arthur Edeson established the perfect tone and mood for evil characters to do their worst. Huston's faithful adaptation of the novel's dialogue realistically presented a world where good and bad people are almost indistinguishable. Bogart, for example, appears to put money before honor. He tells the lying Brigid O'Shaughnessy (Mary Astor), "We didn't believe your story, we believed your money." Only at the film's conclusion does he try to state his real values. "If your partner is killed," Bogart explains to the murderess, "you're supposed to do something about it." The fact that he loves Brigid doesn't change anything. "I'll have some rotten nights after I've sent you over, but that will pass." Above all he lives by a code that won't allow him "to play the sucker for anyone." The most praise, however, went to the superb cast that, in addition to Bogart and Astor, included Peter Lorre, Sydney Greenstreet (his film debut), Elisha Cook, Jr., Jerome Cowan, Barton MacLane, Gladys George, and Ward Bond.

Huston's version of *The Maltese Falcon* gave the gangster formula two major new ingredients. First, to the traditional mobster types and their gangbusting rivals was added a new character: the private eye. Tough, poor, and marginally honest, he walked a thin line between the law and the lawless. Secondly, the film's style started a new trend in Hollywood movies known as *film noir*. As one film historian accurately ex-

In John Huston's version of The Maltese Falcon, *Bogart, as detective Sam Spade, tells the murdering Brigid O'Shaughnessy (Mary Astor) that he's turning her over to the police, with the consoling words, "If they hang you, I'll always remember you."*

plained the style, "The hallmark of *film noir* is its sense of people trapped—trapped in webs of paranoia and fear, unable to tell guilt from innocence, true identity from false. Its villains are attractive and sympathetic, masking greed, misanthropy, malevolence. Its heroes and heroines are weak, confused, susceptible to false impressions. The environment is murky and close, the settings vaguely oppressive. In the end, evil is exposed, though often just barely, and the survival of good remains troubled and ambiguous."

Hollywood got sidetracked before it began mass-producing *film noir* movies. On December 7, 1941, the Japanese attacked Pearl Harbor. The next day America went to war. Movies did their part in the war effort by putting aside social criticisms. This had a direct effect on the gangster formula. Traditional attacks on the country's corrupt politicians, greedy cops, and shady heroes stopped. The spotlight shifted to patriotic gangsters fighting foreign spies.

Vincent Sherman's *All Through the Night* (1942) illustrated the public-spirited mood. Bogart headed a gang that outwits fifth columnists played by Conrad Veidt, Peter Lorre, and Judith Anderson. The script made sure to point out the differences between gangsters and foreign agents in a scene where Bogart is propositioned by Veidt. "It's a pity," the hero is told, ". . . that you and I should oppose each other. We have so much in common. You take what you want and so do we. You have no respect for democracy. Neither do we." Bogart angrily replies, "You're screwy . . . I've been a registered Democrat ever since I could vote. I may not be model citizen No. 1, but I pay my taxes, wait for traffic lights, and buy twenty-four tickets regularly for the policemen's ball. Brother, don't get me mixed up with no league that rubs out innocent little bakers" (a reference to an earlier murder when a German-American refused to aid the Nazi spies). Although the action-packed film lacked logic, Warner Brothers' comic melodrama did well at the box office.

Another 1942 release that was equally patriotic but considerably more powerful was *This Gun for Hire*. Based upon Graham Greene's novel about a hired killer named Philip Raven, the Paramount film altered the original plot to focus on a conspiracy to sell poison gas to Japan. Frank Tuttle's suspenseful direction blended well with the standard gangster dialogue in the Albert Maltz–W. R. Burnett screenplay. And besides turning the film's leads—Alan Ladd and Veronica Lake—into instant stars, *This Gun for Hire* gave the screen the model for psychopathic killers. Vicious, cold-blooded, and extremely clever, Ladd made a memorable impression as the conscienceless hit-man.

Surprisingly, Hollywood didn't follow up with many more patriotic gangster films. One reason given was audience taste. Producers felt that Freudian dramas, musicals, and suspense stories provided better wartime entertainment. Another reason was morale. It didn't help our combat troops to know that back home the syndicate had expanded its gambling operations, moved into the black-market business—illegal sale of domestic products—in Prohibition-like style, and participated in crucial war contracts. Still another reason, never explored in films to this day, is the legendary "Operation Underworld" project. Fearing that the New York and New Jersey docks needed protection from foreign saboteurs, Naval Intelligence allegedly made a deal with the Mafia. Luciano, after being moved to a more comfortable prison, was promised parole after the war in return for his Mafia influence with dockworkers. It was even rumored that the Mafia helped with the Allied landings in and occupation of Sicily and Italy. As a result, the film industry "avoided" hard-hitting attacks on big-time crime. Whatever the reasons, gangster films suffered a setback during World War II.

Then, two weeks before Germany surrendered on May 8, 1945, Monogram Pictures served notice that gangster films were not through. The film biography *Dillinger* rekindled fond memories of the Depression folk heroes.

Alan Ladd and Veronica Lake became the war years' hottest screen lovers. They first paired up in This Gun for Hire, *where Ladd became famous for his portrayal of a cold, calm, calculating killer.*

The Big Sleep *changed the private eye formula and set many of today's most popular gangster conventions. Despite a cryptic plot never fully explained, Bogart's superb performance as Philip Marlowe remains a high point in his career. Lauren Bacall (standing) as the silky, smooth heroine solidified the team (married in real life) as the postwar period's most popular screen lovers.*

Philip Yordan's script, which earned him an Academy Award nomination, sketched out the bank-robbing career of the notorious hoodlum who was killed in a Chicago moviehouse alley in July 1934. Although largely inaccurate, the film itself signaled the changes taking place in Hollywood. For eleven years the Hays office had forbidden any screen biography of Dillinger. Director Max Nosseck's simplistic melodrama, therefore, proved the censors were losing control. *Dillinger* also showed the value of using factual material, real locations, and stock film footage. Known as "new realism" and inspired by the great producer-director Louis De Rochemont, this style, joined to that of the *film noir,* took over the movies of the late forties.

By 1946, film-makers had revived their interest in screen gangsters. But postwar America required specific changes in the formula. Howard Hawks' *The Big Sleep* exemplified some of those changes. Like *The Maltese Falcon,* it was a detective movie starring Bogart and oozing with the stylistic elements of the *film noir*. The key differences were in the characterizations. Gone was Sam Spade's greedy concern for money and reputation. Replacing Spade was novelist Raymond Chandler's detective hero Philip Marlowe, a much more compassionate "shamus," determined to see justice done. Over the next thirty-two years, in movies like *Lady in the Lake* (1947), *Marlowe* (1969), *The Long Goodbye* (1973), *Farewell, My Lovely* (1975), and the remake of *The Big Sleep* (1978), Chandler's hero, not Hammett's, became the ideal figure in the tough-private-eye whodunit. Gone too were the cultured criminals portrayed by Greenstreet and Lorre. The new breed of blackmailers and fashionable gamblers brought the formula back to its close contacts with social reality. The one characterization the late forties kept was the evil woman. What the confusing William Faulkner–Leigh Brackett–Jules Furthman screenplay did was keep you guessing which of the two rich sisters—Lauren Bacall or Martha Vickers—was the killer.

Unlike *The Maltese Falcon*, however, where violence got glossed over, *The Big Sleep* exploited beatings, smashed-up cars, and killings.

Another outstanding 1946 example of Hollywood's preoccupation with gangland violence was *The Killers*. Broadway reporter Mark Hellinger, making his producing debut, worked with screenwriter Anthony Veiler to expand an Ernest Hemingway short story into a shocking film about greed, murder, hit-men, and rival mobsters. In the *film noir* tradition, the characters in this movie live out their brutal existence in barren rooms, dark streets, and shadow-filled diners. Their pals and girl friends are more dangerous to them than the police. Helping to make *The Killers* a top-notch film were newcomers Burt Lancaster, Ava Gardner, and Edmond O'Brien.

Opposite: in Brute Force, *Howard Duff (left) reminds us how lonely imprisonment can become. Burt Lancaster is the leader who brings retribution to the sadistic jailers.*

The Killers *revealed the postwar period's fascination with violence. Burt Lancaster played the innocent guy drawn into the underworld by Ava Gardner, the double-crossing female.*

Credit for *The Killers'* success, however, goes to director Robert Siodmak. He belonged to a group of expatriate European directors—Billy Wilder, Fritz Lang, Otto Preminger, Jules Dassin, Edward Dmytryk—who had changed Hollywood's intellectual climate. Having experienced Hitler's rise to power, they knew firsthand what fear and paranoia could do to people. As a result, Siodmak, along with his fellow émigrés, provided the postwar world with semidocumentary films noted for their harsh reality.

Inspired by the power of *The Killers,* producer Hellinger hired Jules Dassin to direct the most violent prison film ever made, *Brute Force.* The 1947 "big house" drama argued that convicts were being sadistically victimized by cruel prison guards. To protect themselves, the inmates murder stool pigeons, run "kangaroo courts," and stage the screen's bloodiest prison break. "The moral," one film critic joked, "is: don't go to prison; you meet such vile authorities there."

The turning point in this gangster cycle came in August 1947, with Henry Hathaway's *Kiss of Death*. Substituting suspense for violence, screenwriters Ben Hecht and Charles Lederer examined what happens to an ex-gangster who becomes a police informer and tries to go straight. Rather than concentrating on the story itself, director Hathaway, influenced by his training with De Rochemont in semidocumentary film-making, preoccupied himself with authentic location shooting in New York City. The realistic backgrounds gave the overly sentimental plot an added appeal.

Despite the low-key violence in *Kiss of Death*, it is best remembered for one of the most shocking scenes in gangster films. A psychopathic killer seeking revenge straps a paralyzed older woman to her wheelchair and shoves her down a steep stairway to a terrifying death. Richard Widmark's film debut as the unbalanced hoodlum with the hyena-style giggle made him the most menacing gangster of the era.

Eager to capitalize on its new star, Twentieth Century-Fox cast Widmark in another sizzling crime thriller, *The Street With No Name*, a year later. Working with an original story by Harry Kleiner that was skillfully directed by William Keighley, Widmark gave a performance that packed a powerful punch. Yet it revealed that strong film censorship was on the rise again. The plot dealt with the FBI planting an undercover agent in a ruthless gang headed by Widmark. Yet his role avoided the very elements that had won him instant fame: the maniacal laugh and the sadistic exploits. Stressing the "scientific" criminal mind rather than brute force, *The Street With No Name* modernized the forties gangster movie.

Conditions in Hollywood were forcing other changes in the gangster formula. Film-making had become a riskier business. European countries, always a big market for American movies, set up regulations to favor national film industries and cut down on Hollywood's profits. At home, the federal government not only forced the top studios to end their monopolistic control of production, distribution, and exhibition, but also investigated Hollywood's political values. To make matters worse, film attendance fell off greatly because of the rise of television, bowling alleys, and miniature golf. Facing financial collapse, American film-makers returned to the old successful patterns.

John Huston's *Key Largo* (1948) visualized the changes taking place. Collaborating with Richard Brooks on adapting Maxwell Anderson's moralistic 1939 play to the postwar era, Huston assembled a remarkable cast, including Humphrey Bogart, Edward G. Robinson, Claire Trevor, Lauren Bacall, Lionel Barrymore, and Thomas Gomez. The plot showed striking similarities to *The Petrified Forest*. A group of completely different personalities are held captive in a lonely Florida Keys hotel by a onetime kingpin gangster. The familiar Huston theme uses honor, courage, and pity as the means to combat disillusionment.

Strong characterizations marked the high points in *Key Largo*. Bogart was the cynical ex-army officer who at first refuses to fight again, arguing "One Rocco more or less isn't worth dying for." And Robinson, in his last great gangster role as the brutal Rocco, symbolizes the evilness of the underworld. Vicious, arrogant, and dangerous, he pushes his captives too far. One by one, they rebel. Claire Trevor, in her Oscar-winning role as Rocco's boozy gun moll, forces a violent showdown. In the end, idealism triumphs.

Back to back with *Key Largo* was another memorable gangster film, Robert Siodmak's *Cry of The City*. The taut, sternly fashioned melodrama revitalized the familiar story about two former childhood buddies—one a cop (Victor Mature) and the other a killer (Richard Conte)—who meet in a predictable showdown. Although the plot simply involves

In Key Largo, Bogart plays the disillusioned ex-army officer trying to escape from life's harsh realities. But he discovers there is no way to avoid evil. From left to right, William Haade, Lionel Barrymore, Bogart, Harry Lewis, Thomas Gomez, Dan Seymour, and Lauren Bacall.

a manhunt through New York's tough neighborhoods, Siodmak's expertly directed cast breathed new life into old standbys like the mobster's kid brother, sobbing mother, shyster lawyer, and innocent girl.

Equally important in Hollywood's 1948 gangster revival was Abraham Polonsky's *Force of Evil*. Stories about ghetto kids being trapped by racketeers and corrupt politicians were not unique. What made *Force of Evil* special was the stress the film placed on moral decay. John Garfield's exciting performance as the young syndicate lawyer corrupted by blind ambition helped restore a social consciousness to movies. Crime again became tied to America's misdirected emphasis on material success.

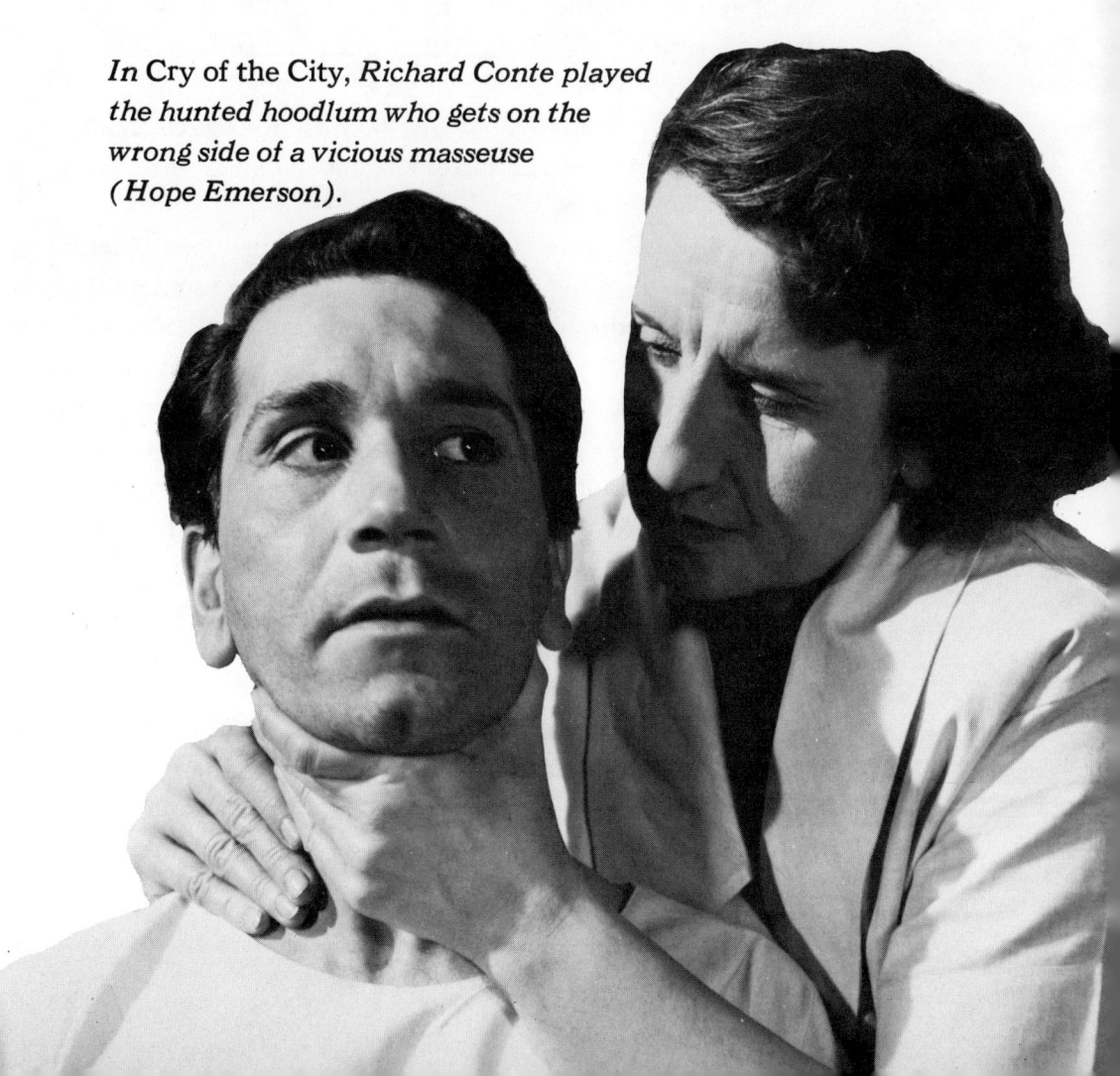

In Cry of the City, *Richard Conte played the hunted hoodlum who gets on the wrong side of a vicious masseuse (Hope Emerson).*

Criss Cross (1949) exploited still another aspect of criminal corruption, the gangster-triangle theme. The Daniel Fuchs screenplay effectively dramatized what happened to a decent, honest guard (Burt Lancaster) who is tricked by his ex-wife (Yvonne de Carlo) and her new husband (Dan Duryea) into robbing an armored car. Under Siodmak's intelligent direction, the tired formula had a rebirth. Scenes describing the bank robbery plans are cleverly staged and lead to a thrilling conclusion as the characters one by one turn violently on each other.

The highlight of the postwar cycle also proved to be the decade's last great underworld film, Raoul Walsh's *White Heat*. Called by the *New York Times* "the acme of the gangster-prison film," the story focused on a neurotic hoodlum (James Cagney) whose cutthroat gang is finally destroyed by the Treasury Department. Virginia Kellogg's original story, earning her an Academy Award nomination, gave Walsh his chance to mix the era's matter-of-fact violence with old-time gangland conventions.

For the last time, audiences saw the brilliant Cagney as an unforgettable gangster. His Cody Jarrett, a homicidal paranoic with an Oedipus complex, was electrifying. In one scene, he sits on his mother's lap after having an epileptic fit and she (Margaret Wycherly) rubs the madman's head. Done by anyone else, the episode would have been laughed off the screen. Another superb moment occurs in the prison dining room when Jarrett gets word that his mother has been killed. Cagney at first looks down, internalizing his grief. Then the rage and grief build and he throws a wild fit, screaming, crying, fighting until forcibly subdued. But the most memorable moment comes at the end when Cagney, wounded and cornered on top of an oil tank, grins at his pursuers shouting, "Made it, Ma, top of the world," and commits suicide by firing his gun into the oil tank.

White Heat was a fitting conclusion to the forties. Just as Walsh's *High Sierra* had been Hollywood's final tribute to the individualism of old-time gangsters, so Cody Jarrett's violent death ended the days of the mindless killers. In the decades to follow, types like Jarrett would appear periodically, but a new image would hold the spotlight: the organization man.

Raoul Walsh's White Heat *contained many outstanding gangster conventions: the big heist, a prison break, rival hoodlums, and spectacular action scenes. At its core, however, was the mother fixation that drove Cody Jarrett (Cagney) mad. Margaret Wycherly, modeled after the infamous "Ma" Barker, gave a remarkable performance.*

1950
THE SYNDICATE YEARS
1959

By 1950, Hollywood found itself in a life-and-death struggle for survival. The major cause was economics. Studios forced by the Justice Department to give up their large theater empires no longer had a guaranteed market. In the past, 80 percent of the big studios' film output made money. Now only one picture in ten returned a profit. Consequently, fewer films were produced. Less work brought massive unemployment. Studio after studio disbanded its roster of contract players, directors, technicians, and producers. Worse, television's free entertainment brought movie house attendance to all-time lows. Theaters closed by the thousands. Another crucial problem facing the film industry was the Red Scare. A witch-hunt for communists, arising out of the Cold War and the Korean conflict, reached alarming proportions by the start of the decade. Led by Senator Joseph McCarthy, self-appointed watchdogs unfairly victimized the entertainment industry. A nation paralyzed with fear forced outspoken film-makers into prison terms or exile abroad. Still another problem was America's growing concern over Hollywood's moral influence on its citizens. Powerful groups investigated how films exploited violence and sex, allegedly producing juvenile delinquents and criminals.

It is in this context that the uneven quality of fifties gangster movies must be understood. During this troubled era, the gangster movie, like every other Hollywood formula, needed creative artists to develop new approaches. But that required time.

Warner Brothers' *Caged* (1950) started the decade off on a fresh path. Ever since *The Big House* in 1930, prison films had protested the oppressive conditions that humiliated male inmates. This time the plot focused on a nineteen-year-old woman (Eleanor Parker) whose husband dies robbing a gas station. Although innocent, she is sent to jail and experiences the emotionally deadening effects of sadistic guards, vicious cellmates, and prison violence. The obvious attempt to balance the film's ringing social attack by including a humane warden

Above: Agnes Moorehead played the humanitarian warden in Caged. Her sympathy for the innocent Eleanor Parker does not prevent the prisoner from becoming bitter and corrupt in jail. *Below:* The Asphalt Jungle presented a frightening vision of the modern city. Marilyn Monroe was Louis Calhern's "niece" (censors in 1950 forbade the word "mistress"). Betrayed by her in the end, the crooked lawyer quips, "You did pretty well, considering."

(Agnes Moorehead) did not offset the audience's sympathy for the prisoners. The fact that the heroine emerged from her ordeal a bitter, corrupted person reinforced the gangster film's close ties with social reality.

It was scriptwriter Virginia Kellogg who provided director John Cromwell with the terrifying facts. By "doing time" under a false name in several institutions, she discovered first-hand the desperate conditions of prison life. "In one prison," a film historian reported, "Miss Kellogg noted how a girl had her head shaved because she had attempted an escape or she had committed an act of lesbianism; in another, she saw prisoners beat spoons in anger on their metal dishes at a Christmas party because they had not received presents. She came to understand the agonized struggle for a woman to raise a baby or use lipstick, the evil matrons who used their privileges to obtain bribes; the gossip, laughter, and misery of the 'bullpens' or dormitories; the tension when a hated superintendent came by." Director Cromwell, together with cinematographer Carl Guthrie, then turned the dramatic material into a brutal attack on the penal system. It was a theme the fifties would use again and again.

The changing face of gangster movies was further shaped a few weeks after *Caged* was released by MGM's *The Asphalt Jungle*. W. R. Burnett, whose novels had given Hollywood such film classics as *Little Caesar* and *High Sierra*, now gave the screen the model for all future heist thrillers. Scripted by Ben Maddow and John Huston, the scenario dealt with a group of criminals recruited for a million-dollar jewel robbery. What made the movie so compelling was director Huston's characterizations and casting: Sam Jaffee as the debonair jewel thief with a weakness for young girls; Sterling Hayden, the ill-fated strong-arm man wanting just one big job to get him free of the corrupt city; Louis Calhern, the crooked lawyer who finances the robbery from a nonexistent bankroll; and Marilyn Monroe, the dumb but conniving blonde mistress.

The Asphalt Jungle brought special attention to what would become a major concern of the gangster film—the highly placed criminal who masterminds underworld operations. By selecting Calhern for the crucial role, giving him a cynical philosophy that stated "Crime is merely a left-handed form of human behavior," Huston made audiences rethink their attitudes toward crime. The film's realistic impact earned the writer-director two more Oscar nominations and the 1950 Screen Directors Guild Award.

While gangster films worked on refining their image in 1950, a young Tennessee senator, Estes Kefauver, convinced his associates that it was in the national interest to expose the role of organized crime in interstate commerce. Building his case carefully, he investigated criminal operations across the country and traced their roots from Prohibition days through the Depression and up to the widespread rise of gambling casinos. To focus national attention on the unholy alliance among dishonest businessmen, unethical public officials, and the underworld, Senator Kefauver televised the public hearings. The Committee's final report in 1951 concluded that a national crime syndicate operated mainly by the Mafia existed in many of America's large cities.

Although the sensational hearings had little effect on crime prevention and distorted the Mafia's influence, the Kefauver Committee produced two major effects. First, organized crime began channeling its money into legitimate "front" operations. Second, the public realized that the underworld was bigger than ever.

Warner Brothers' *The Enforcer,* released in January 1951, was one of the first films to capitalize on the Committee's work. Directed by Bretaigne Windust, the plot followed a crusading district attorney's efforts to destroy Murder Inc. Martin Rackin's informative screenplay told of star witnesses' "accidentally" dying, hired killers on a national scale, and a murder's "graveyard." Sharp performances were turned in by

Humphrey Bogart as the unrelenting D.A.; Zero Mostel, the pathetic punk who tries to join the gang; and Ted De Corsia, the onetime tough guy who turns informer.

The Enforcer proved to be a turning point in several ways for gangster movies. Nostalgically, it ended the fourteen-year relationship between Bogart and Warner Brothers. It also climaxed the efforts by long-established directors to influence the formula's new images. From 1951 on, fresher directors with more violent and sexually oriented styles took over.

Helping drive out old screen gangsters was Jack Webb's popular 1952 television series "Dragnet." Ironically, the idea originated from a 1948 movie, *He Walked by Night,* in which Webb played a hard-working cop. He decided to expand the role into a radio series that same year, which in turn inspired the video show. "Dragnet" stressed both family entertainment and a realistic attitude toward crime fighting. As producer-director-star, Webb downplayed violence and concentrated on strong characterizations.

Pickup on South Street, released in 1953, was one response to television's approach. Scripted and directed by Sam Fuller, it offered an overabundance of violence and a simplified story line. Richard Widmark starred as a brutal hoodlum who accidentally steals information belonging to foreign agents and ends up smashing a communist spy ring. Not since *The Public Enemy* had women received the harsh treatment afforded co-stars Jean Peters and Thelma Ritter. The former plays Widmark's girl friend, thus making her eligible for a black eye, a concussion, and periodic beatings. The latter, cast as a misguided stoolie, gets her head blown off.

Pickup on South Street's excessive violence overshadowed Fuller's remarkable visual style. Critics attacked the film's sensationalism, labeling the director a fascist. Only with passing years have viewers begun to appreciate his mobile camera work and the artistic skill with which Fuller expresses himself.

Much more appreciated was Fritz Lang's *The Big Heat.*

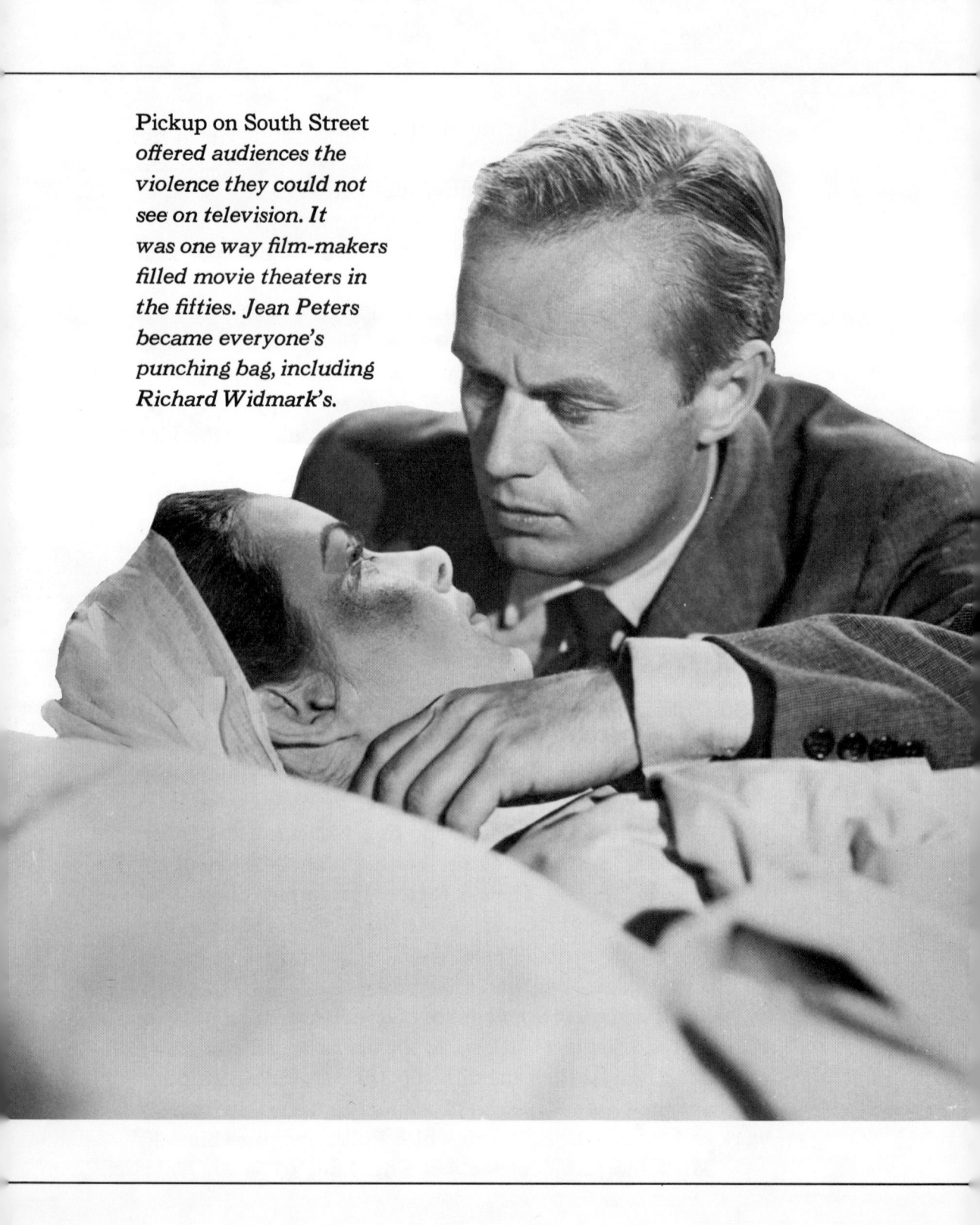

Pickup on South Street *offered audiences the violence they could not see on television. It was one way film-makers filled movie theaters in the fifties. Jean Peters became everyone's punching bag, including Richard Widmark's.*

Contributing to The Big Heat's *success was director Lang's stress on the effects of violence. The most talked about scene dealt with a sadistic thug (Lee Marvin) throwing boiling coffee in his moll's face. Gloria Grahame, shown here, returned the favor later on.*

While just as brutal as *Pickup on South Street,* the 1953 film effectively mixed violence and sex in a powerful attack on syndicate activities. Lang's genius was in getting audiences to identify with the hero's feelings about organized crime. Opening with a policeman's suicide, the brilliant *film noir* director showed the results of violence. Glenn Ford as the hate-filled cop seeking revenge for his wife's violent murder got viewer sympathy as he battled corrupt politicians, sadistic thugs, and powerful big-city bosses. The feeling throughout *The Big Heat* was that corruption existed everywhere.

The next imaginative approach to the gangster formula was Don Siegel's *Riot in Cell Block 11*. Based on Dick Collins' original script about a prison revolt, the 1954 film rejected the standard clichés. Characterizations get bypassed in favor of the social issue. Two opposing sides wrestle with the crisis created by poorly paid guards, meaningless rehabilitation programs, bad food, inadequate living conditions, and unreasonable politicians. Neither the prisoners nor the public officials have a united front. Good and bad men are in both camps. Although sadistic acts occur throughout the movie, violence is presented as necessary to the story's theme. Lending authenticity are Folsom Prison locations, little-known actors, the absence of women, and the pessimistic ending.

Riot in Cell Block 11 became Siegel's first important film. A former cutter at Warner Brothers, he used his superb editing skills to turn this low-budget movie into one of the most realistic prison films ever made.

Siegel's film was closely followed by Elia Kazan's *On The Waterfront.* Played against the background of the New York waterfront, the Budd Schulberg script concentrated on dock union corruption. The strong drama reminded audiences of the social criticisms raised in *Angels With Dirty Faces* and *Force of Evil.* But director Kazan made his hero's moral awakening very autobiographical. Terry Malloy's painful realization that informing on men who rule through fear and violence is a de-

Right: Riot in Cell Block 11 *gave the fifties a realistic look at prison conditions. Neville Brand (above) became the first of many violent, lonely men created by director Don Siegel. As the con who fights both the officials and fellow inmate Leo Gordon, Brand proved to be an impressive anti-hero. Below: Elia Kazan's* On the Waterfront *was a strong, controversial look at graft on the New York docks. Marlon Brando portrayed the young worker who dared to challenge the syndicate's corrupt practices. Karl Malden (left) and Eva Marie Saint console the battered Brando.*

cent act produced varied reactions. Kazan had recently testified against alleged communists in Hollywood and been labeled an "informer." Consequently, many people wondered if the film was an apology for the director's actions or a sizzling attack on syndicate vice.

No one wondered about the film's artistic merit. It became the most honored gangster movie yet made. Among its countless awards were eight Oscars, including ones for best production, best actor (Marlon Brando), best supporting actress (Eva Marie Saint), best black-and-white photography (Boris Kauffman), and best story and screenplay (Schulberg). This milestone film also provided Brando with what may be his greatest performance.

In May 1955, Robert Aldrich's *Kiss Me Deadly* revealed the McCarthy Era's effect on the detective formula. The Mike Hammer hero created by novelist Mickey Spillane differed significantly from past private eyes like Sam Spade and Philip Marlowe. Earlier detectives followed ethical codes. Hammer made up his own rules. They rarely became violent. Hammer was more brutal than the criminals he pursued. Although first brought to the screen in Harry Essex's 1953 potboiler *I, The Jury*, the Hammer image got its best outing under Aldrich's unflinching look at a violent society. Refusing to moralize, the director showed the private eye as a man disgusted by his environment and thus free to act as he chooses. Ralph Meeker portrayed the avenging shamus as smashing anyone who stands in his way.

The issue of a corrupt society got wider coverage later that year in Phil Karlson's *The Phenix City Story*. An aroused public eager to see the events surrounding the sordid murder of the 1954 Democratic nominee for attorney general of Alabama found the low-budget film surprisingly realistic. The Crane Wilbur–Daniel Mainwaring scenario featured actual interviews with citizens who knew the late Albert Patterson as well as a detailed account of the syndicate's gambling and vice operations. Resembling the semidocumentary approach used in

On The Waterfront, the film vividly showed a corrupt city paralyzed by fear.

The gangster event of 1956 was Stanley Kubrick's *The Killing.* Following the big heist formula developed by *White Heat* and *The Asphalt Jungle,* the young director co-scripted a tense and engrossing story about a two-million-dollar race-track robbery. Kubrick, in his first important film, revealed his gifts for characterization and editing. The gang consisted of "losers," all needing money and doomed from the outset. Their big dreams are contrasted sharply with their pathetic lives. While excitement builds in the planning stages, Kubrick and his editor, Betty Steinberg, introduce superb cutting skills to portray the actual robbery. And in true caper tradition, the film ends on a brutal and ironic note.

Audiences waited nearly two years for the next major gangster highlight, Robert Wise's *I Want to Live.* Aided by

Susan Hayward reenacted the ordeal of call-girl Barbara Graham in I Want to Live. *The central issue was capital punishment. Had Graham been railroaded? Was the state justified in executing a human being? Did the system operate humanely?*

Walter Wanger, who produced *Caged,* the director expertly reenacted the nightmare of Barbara Graham. Mother of three, prostitute, and dope addict, she fell in with a dangerous gang, got accused of murdering an elderly widow, found herself unable to overturn her conviction, and died in the San Quentin gas chamber. Susan Hayward's Oscar-winning performance reached its peak during the second half of the film, which dealt with the condemned woman's death house ordeal. Despite both the picture's popularity and the outstanding issues raised, this 1958 melodrama provided the last important woman's role in gangster movies for nearly a decade.

Public attention, in the meantime, was directed to newspaper accounts stating that close to sixty leading mobsters had gathered in Apalachin, New York, the previous year for an underworld summit. Senator John McClellan led a Select Senate Committee investigation on how these mobsters had infiltrated labor and business.

Television took advantage of the nation's concerns to regain ground it had lost to the violent gangster movies. A 1958 two-part drama about Chicago crime during the thirties resulted the following year in the enormously popular TV series *The Untouchables.* Robert Stack starred as the incorruptible, hard-hitting Eliot Ness, who headed an aggressive special FBI team against organized crime. Credited by some historians as the most violent television series ever made, *The Untouchables* matched Hollywood's new interest in gangster biographies.

Starting in 1957 with Don Siegel's *Baby-Face Nelson,* the late fifties featured a rash of violent, historical reenactments of old-time hoodlums like "Machine Gun" Kelly, Bonnie Parker, and "Pretty Boy" Floyd.

Typical of the new cycle was Richard Wilson's semidocumentary *Al Capone* in 1959. Striving for realism, the Malvin Wald–Henry Greenberg scenario depicted the psychological problems Capone faced as he rose from a two-bit bouncer to the kingpin of Chicago crime. Director Wilson took pains to show what happened to Capone following his conviction for income tax evasion in 1931, the eight-year prison term that mentally destroyed the cowardly mobster, and his subsequent death in 1947. What made this low-budget film so special was Rod Steiger's masterly performance. Trained in the method acting style popularized by Brando, Steiger showed audiences just how sick a man Capone actually was.

As the fifties closed, the gangster film seemed headed for better times. Its formula had given rise to fresh ideas and new talents. Violent movies were drawing fans away from television. The question everyone asked was, "Would the suddenly found popularity last?"

Rod Steiger starred in the gangster biography Al Capone.

Aided by a fine supporting cast that included Nehemiah Persoff and Martin Balsam, the film's impressive documentary style deromanticized the Capone legend.

1960
LOST BOUNDARIES
1969

The sixties were the replacement years. Television became America's favorite pastime. It took over filmdom's factory system of production. Crime serials like "Peter Gunn," "77 Sunset Strip," "Perry Mason," and "Lineup," once the standard B-movies, now became daily TV fare. As the decade moved on, these action-packed shows were replaced by parodies of the bang-stab-plop formula. Viewers tuned in nightly to "The Man from U.N.C.L.E.," "I Spy," "Batman," "The Green Hornet," and "The Avengers." Critics didn't know whether to laugh at the tongue-in-cheek violence or attack viewer encouragement of screen mayhem. By the end of the sixties, TV crime serials had grown both in number and in seriousness. Among audience favorites were "Name of The Game," "Mod Squad," "Hawaii Five-0," "Adam-12," and "The Lawyers." Television now found itself under attack for corrupting the country's morals. In 1968, for example, the National Commission on Civil Disorders singled out TV's unrealistic picture of American life as one of the causes of the urban riots enflaming the country.

Stripped of its uniqueness, the film industry struck back in the sixties with multimillion dollar movies, "blockbusters." Independent producers replaced studios in financing and making the extravaganzas. Agents, stars, and unions became the power-brokers. They worked closely with conglomerates like Gulf and Western to creat a new Hollywood. Higher costs and greater risks required new rules. Old movie codes were modernized with a rating system. Film content got in step with the era's revolutionary attitudes on sexual freedom, drugs, civil rights, student protests, and antiwar sentiment.

Yet, as the decade began, gangster movies gave no sign that they knew times were changing. Only two themes interested the formula's artists.

The first theme concerned biographies. Better than most was Budd Boetticher's *The Rise and Fall of "Legs" Diamond* in 1960. Set during the Depression, the semifactual screenplay chronicled the life of New York's flashiest and deadliest gangster. Ray Danton interpreted the onetime dancer as an egotistical mobster destroyed by his own vanity. Producer-director Richard Wilson's *Pay or Die*, also in 1960, showed New York crime in another light. Based upon the life of detective Joseph Petrosino, the brutal script dramatized the century's first efforts to fight Mafia activities. Ernest Borgnine starred as a brave Italian-American fighting to free New York's little Italy of old-world terrors.

Films about the syndicate reflected the other concern of the early sixties. Two different approaches surfaced with *Murder, Inc.* (1960) and *Underworld, U.S.A.* (1961). The former

Violent gunfights and strong acting highlighted Burt Balaban's Murder, Inc. *Peter Falk (left) played the vicious killer Abe Reles who terrorized the mob's enemies, including Stuart Whitman and May Britt.*

was producer-director Burton Balaban's low-budget adaptation of assistant D.A. Burton Turkus' book. Relying heavily on the public's familiarity with the actual events and personalities, Balaban focused attention on the notorious killer Abe Reles. His turning informer allows Turkus to smash Louis "Lepke" Buchalter's Brooklyn mob. As Reles, Peter Falk provided the film's major highlights.

Producer-director-writer Sam Fuller tackled organized crime differently in *Underworld, U.S.A.* While maintaining a realistic atmosphere, he ignored well-known events, choosing instead to present a sordid picture of kingpin mobsters using charities as "fronts." Cliff Robertson enlarged the anti-hero character developed by Fuller in *Pickup on South Street*. Seeking revenge for his father's murder, Robertson becomes a double agent, working for and against the syndicate, but feeling no loyalty to either the FBI or the underworld. His warped ends justify his violent means. The only way shown to destroy the syndicate's vice operations is to wipe out the crime lords themselves.

By 1962, however, the B-formula seemed worn out. Television now became the primary source for the quickly made, low-budget action story. Badly misunderstood and underrated, the gangster film no longer appealed to a nation frightened by world problems.

John Frankenheimer's *Birdman of Alcatraz* (1962) courageously suggested that prison stories did indeed relate to America's renewed interests in human rights. This compelling film addressed the issue of rehabilitation. Using as its source Thomas E. Gaddis' biography, the story opens in 1909 with convicted murderer Robert Stroud beginning what was to be a twelve-year prison term. But a violent prison fight results in Stroud killing a guard, being sentenced to death, and then having the sentence commuted to life imprisonment in solitary confinement. Over the next fifty years we see a once-hardened convict change character through his absorption in the study and care of birds. Nevertheless, director Frankenheimer's realistic picture of one man's suffering, loneliness, and achievement proved unpopular with audiences preoccupied with larger issues. The film did, however, provide Burt Lancaster with one of his finest roles.

Except for Don Siegel's memorable remake of *The Killers* in 1964, the mid-sixties ignored serious gangster themes. Filmmakers opted for blockbuster parodies of the detective formula. Britain led the way. Terence Young gave us Ian Fleming's James Bond in *Dr. No* (1963). Blake Edwards offered the bumbling Inspector Clouseau in *The Pink Panther* (1964). For America, not to be outdone, Daniel Mann satirized the super-sleuths with the outrageous *Our Man Flint* (1966), while the flamboyant Matt Helm surfaced in Phil Karlson's *The Silencers* (1966). Actors like Sean Connery, Peter Sellers, James Coburn, and Dean Martin won viewer support as they battled worldwide conspiracies, used remarkable technological gadgets, and romanced exotic women.

Then came the summer of 1967 and everything changed. Three new gangster films appeared, differing widely in content and style. Yet they shared one important characteristic: a newfound freedom from clichés, conventions, and censorship.

Producer-director Roger Corman started things off with his first big-budget film, *The St. Valentine's Day Massacre*. Mounted with some magnificently reconstructed settings, the Howard Browne screenplay detailed the gory events of February 14, 1929, on Chicago's North Clark Street when Al Capone's mob murdered seven members of the Bugs Moran gang. The reconstructed Capone-Moran feud contrasted the public and private lives of racketeers. As gangsters waged machine-gun battles in the street, their bosses posed as respectable businessmen no different from other honest citizens. Although Corman's semidocumentary style failed to impress critics who attacked the movie's acting, direction, and construction, young people identified with the picture's cynical values.

Bigger, better, and far more controversial was Arthur Penn's explosive film *Bonnie and Clyde*. The director wanted a story about outcasts that would act as a commentary on the antisocial, revolutionary spirit sweeping the sixties. The sordid careers of the historical Bonnie Parker and Clyde Barrow—bank robbers and killers—served his needs ideally. Roaming through Texas and Oklahoma from 1931 until their death on

Gene Hackman (left) plays Buck Barrow, drawn into a whirlpool of crime during the Depression by his infamous brother Clyde Barrow (Warren Beatty), in Arthur Penn's violent film Bonnie and Clyde.

The psychological gangster film reached its peak with Bonnie and Clyde. Warren Beatty and Faye Dunaway starred as the leaders of the notorious Barrow gang who made headlines during the Great Depression of the thirties.

May 23, 1934, the outlaws in Penn's movie became pop-heroes. Bank robber Clyde (Warren Beatty) and his cigar-smoking girl friend Bonnie (Faye Dunaway) capture sheriffs, terrorize bank tellers, and grab headlines with their daring, reckless, and often senseless crimes. No matter how violent their deeds, the David Newman–Robert Benton script presents the pair as sympathetic and attractive figures. Bonnie and Clyde came off as modern-day Robin Hoods, alive and at odds with an amoral society. "What I'm really trying to say through the figure of the outcast," explained Penn, "is that a society has a mirror in its outcasts." To a generation critical of its institutions and revolted by the mindless everyday violence of the sixties, the film rang true. Criminals seemed to be the products of a corrupt society. Adding to the film's powerful appeal were the director's splendid techniques. Moods of violence blended with those of comedy and pathos, suggesting a fantasy world destroyed only at the end when the notorious outlaws are ambushed and slaughtered.

Bonnie and Clyde might have been just another misunderstood gangster movie if not for the critical reaction to Penn's celebration of violence. A *New York Times* review claimed it was "a cheap piece of bald-faced slapstick comedy that treats the hideous depredations of that sleazy moronic pair as though they were . . . full of fun and frolic. . . ." Fearing that the influential review might kill the film's chances for success, Warner Brothers started a heavy advertising campaign. Critics took sides. Some praised every bloody act in the movie. Others condemned the film's many historical inaccuracies. One reviewer, writing for *Newsweek,* first attacked *Bonnie and Clyde* as a "squalid shoot-'em for the moron trade," and then reversed himself the following week, stating that his review was "grossly unfair and regrettably inaccurate." The critical debate produced widespread interest and audiences lined up to see the controversial film.

The growing storm over movie violence increased a month later with John Boorman's *Point Blank*. Filled with riddles and unanswered questions suggestive of *The Big Sleep*, the plot dealt with one man's vendetta against the Organization. Flashbacks and flashforwards tell of a killer (Lee Marvin) double-crossed and left for dead who miraculously survives and wages a brutal revenge. Avoiding the standard locations of Los Angeles and San Francisco, Boorman presents a fresh look at a modern-day bureaucraticized syndicate. The director was also well-served by his cast, including Marvin, Carroll O'Connor, Angie Dickinson, and Keenan Wynn.

These three violent movies brought a fresh outcry for film censorship. But Hollywood, by now, knew how to fight such protests. The industry, as it has so often done in the past, switched attention to crime-busters instead of outlaws.

Leading the way in 1968 was Don Siegel's *Madigan*. The serious, hard-hitting melodrama of a New York City manhunt for a killer served as the pretext for a moral debate on police methods. The Police Commissioner (Henry Fonda) insisted his men follow the rules. No one, he argued, had the right to break the law. Detectives Madigan (Richard Widmark) and Bonaro (Harry Guardino) argued otherwise. Lonely, antisocial, and violent men, they must lie, cheat, and disobey their superiors to protect society. In the end Madigan gets killed, leaving audiences to wonder about the price one pays to fight crime. Just as the critics attacked *Bonnie and Clyde* for making outlaws sympathetic people, they accused *Madigan* of justifying police brutality.

The debate over police methods continued later that year in Peter Yates' first American film, *Bullitt*. Steve McQueen, cast as a dedicated San Francisco police lieutenant who puts integrity above his career, forces us to ask ourselves, "How should crime be fought?" Ordered by his politically ambitious superior (Robert Vaughn) not to interfere in a Senate committee investigation, McQueen refuses and eventually kills the

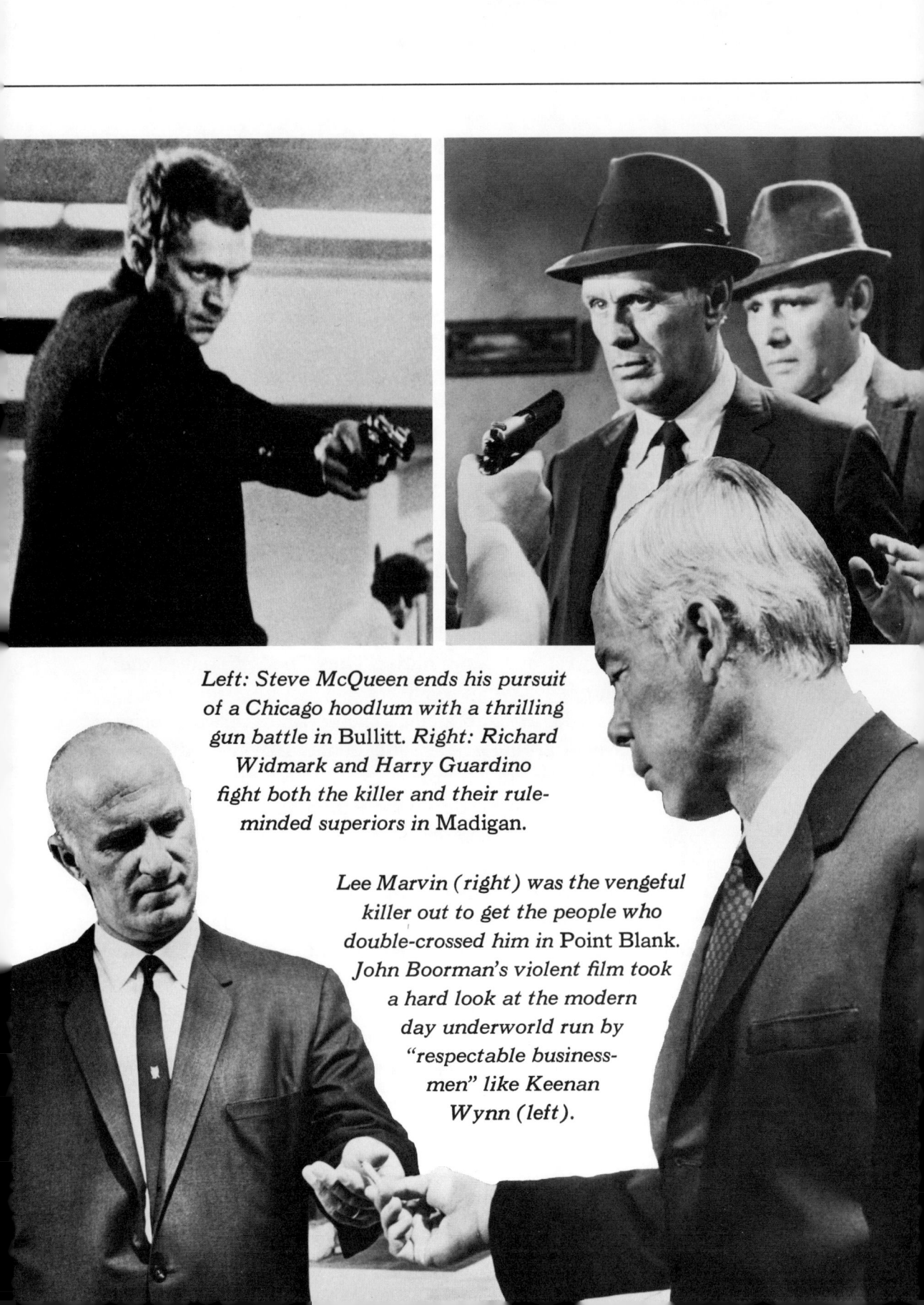

Left: Steve McQueen ends his pursuit of a Chicago hoodlum with a thrilling gun battle in Bullitt. *Right: Richard Widmark and Harry Guardino fight both the killer and their rule-minded superiors in* Madigan.

Lee Marvin (right) was the vengeful killer out to get the people who double-crossed him in Point Blank. *John Boorman's violent film took a hard look at the modern day underworld run by "respectable businessmen" like Keenan Wynn (left).*

star witness. The lawman's world, shown both in *Madigan* and *Bullitt,* is filled with cops who are corrupt, ruthless, and brutal people. Audiences wondered why? Does society make policemen behave this way? Is it because living and working with criminals changes an individual? Adding to *Bullitt*'s top-notch suspense was Frank P. Keller's Oscar-winning editing of an eleven-minute car chase that concludes with a spectacular crash.

Gangster films underwent other dramatic changes in 1968. Economic woes plus the need for new audiences inspired MGM to star black performers in escapist films. Impressed by what a Richard Stark novel did for *Point Blank,* the studio adapted another Stark book for Gordon Flemyng's *The Split.* Jim Brown masterminded a gang of professional crooks who pull off a $500,000 heist. Publicity campaigns made the point that "in his [Jim Brown's] violent underworld they judge a man by the color of the money he steals!" Although Flemyng lacked Boorman's directorial skills, he did make good use of racial jokes and strong personalities. Thus *The Split* paved the way for future black gangster stories.

As the sixties drew to a close, the new film-making techniques, business arrangements, and updated themes affected every gangster film. The best example was Martin Ritt's *The Brotherhood* (1968). Produced for Paramount by actor Kirk Douglas, the original screenplay by Lewis John Carlino was a moving tale about changing values in a Mafia family. Douglas starred as a middle-aged syndicate leader who violently opposes the Organization's new multi-ethnic board and legitimate businesses. Replaced by his brother (Alex Cord), Douglas still refuses to follow syndicate orders and has to be killed. Cord is given the "hit," establishing the fact that the good of the syndicate is more important than family ties. Effective casting, original touches, and realistic locations resulted in a powerful film about the rise of a modern underworld.

Despite the newfound freedom, new artists, and new conventions, Hollywood worried about its future. Fresh ideas did not insure quality films. Pressure groups like the National Italian-American League to Combat Defamation and the Americans of Italian Descent objected to a film like *The Brotherhood*, claiming it was "a disgraceful spectacle that denigrates, slurs, defames, and stigmatizes twenty-two million Americans of Italian descent." Industry and audience alike wondered what would come next.

Martin Ritt's The Brotherhood *dramatized the conflict that syndicate members have with progress and family ties. Kirk Douglas, an aging gangster, puts revenge on a stoolie (Luther Adler) over personal safety and business.*

1970
STRICTLY BUSINESS
1978

The seventies posed special problems for gangster movies. It was an almost-anything-goes time. Rapid changes in censorship, technology, business methods, and social values made it difficult to measure what audiences wanted. Some experts argued for escapism. The public needed it. Political upheavals like the Vietnam War and Watergate added to the nation's woes over energy and economics. Jimmy Carter won the presidency on the campaign theme that there is a "hunger in this country to get back those precious things we lost." During the decade, Americans went on a nostalgia binge. Film retrospectives gave aging adults and youngsters a fresh look at the old values. Former greats like Robinson and Cagney were honored by the movie industry.

Coexisting with Hollywood's make-believe past was the contemporary hunger for realistic, violent, action-packed stories. Film profits were tied to murders, beatings, brawls, rapes, and other forms of mayhem. Confusion arose when the audiences hypocritically debated the alleged connection between screen violence and national crime. Criticism of TV shows reached new heights. Shows like "McCloud," "McMillan and Wife," "Columbo," "Cannon," "Mannix," and "Baretta" produced storms of protest from concerned citizens. Senate hearings were held on TV violence and the complaints continued to pour in. An aroused public began to believe that the steady diet of film and TV violence was directly tied to the rising crime rate in the streets. Narcotics, prostitution, extortion, gambling, and loansharking were flourishing and apparently out of control. Cities once more housed areas where neither life nor property were safe. Ignorant of how to fight the rising crime rate, civic leaders made violent movies and TV crime serials the scapegoat. Being businessmen as well as entertainers, film-makers wondered what to do.

Producer-director Roger Corman thought he found the answer in 1970 with his box-office hit *Bloody Mama*. The semibiographical script followed the sordid trail of Kate "Ma"

Barker and her dim-witted sons during the Depression. Convinced that money made you free, she terrorized the South with holdups, kidnappings, and murders until her violent death on January 16, 1935. Comparisons between *Bloody Mama* and *Bonnie and Clyde* were inescapable. Both were nostalgic, violent movies about Depression outlaws, handsomely mounted and authentically presented. But they had two particular differences. Shelley Winters' "Ma" Barker was no attractive, sympathetic figure. Fat, vulgar, and cruel, she looked as frightening as she acted. And unlike Penn's outlaws, the Barker gang was killed because it threatened society, not because its members were "rebels."

Trying to tap audience reactions, film-makers throughout the seventies reworked the Depression formula, stressing the sensational and ignoring the importance of context and relationship. Typical was John Milius' *Dillinger* (1973). Making his directorial debut, he scripted a thinly veiled copy of Penn's classic techniques. The notorious bank robber (well-played by Warren Oates) finds himself pursued by the publicity-conscious Melvin Purvis (Ben Johnson), head of the FBI's Midwestern office. Before Dillinger is gunned down, Purvis gets a chance to capture or kill such infamous outlaws as "Machine Gun" Kelly, "Pretty Boy" Floyd, and "Baby Face" Nelson. Another sexploitation example was Steve Carver's *Big Bad Mama* (1974). The Roger Corman protégé reworked the Barker formula, cast Angie Dickinson as a sexually active, violent matriarch of two daughters, and filmed an amoral tale of murderous bank robbers fated for a bloody death.

Not all films imitating *Bonnie and Clyde* competed for more sensational sights and sounds. The outstanding exception was Robert Altman's compassionate social drama about the Depression, *Thieves Like Us* (1974). The story, based on a 1937 novel by Edward Anderson, had been told once before in Nicholas Ray's 1948 film, *They Live By Night*. Yet in Altman's hands, it became a vital commentary on rootlessness in

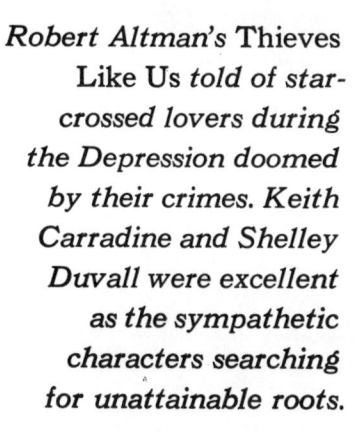

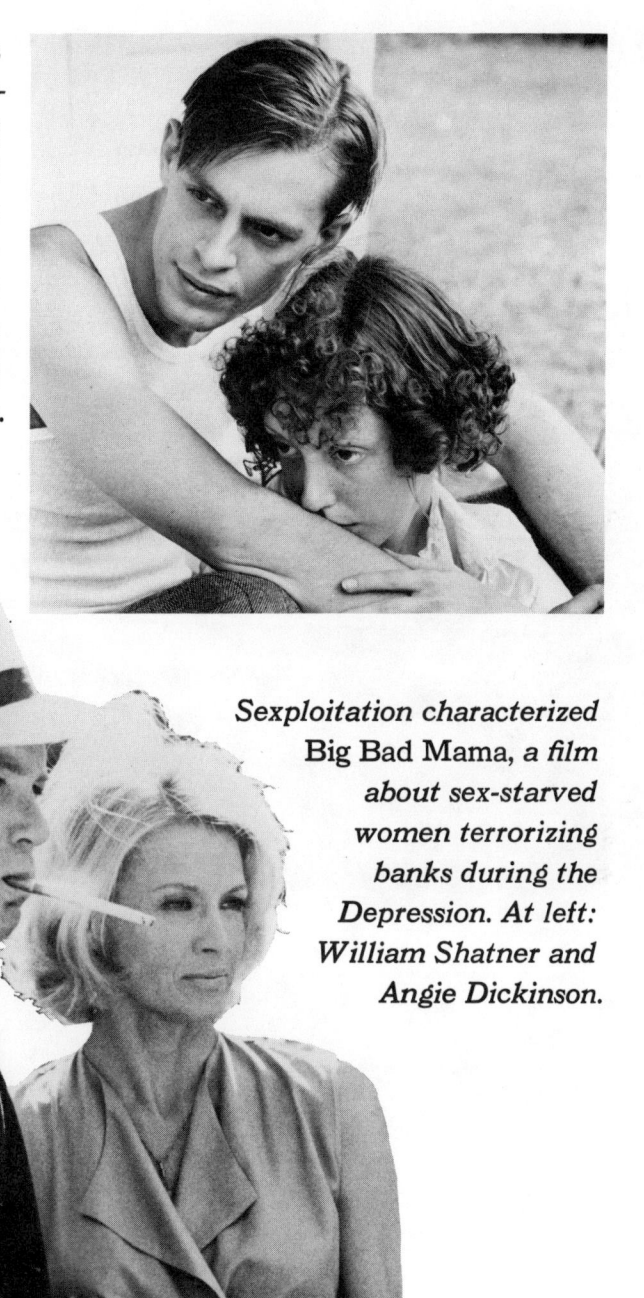

Robert Altman's Thieves Like Us *told of star-crossed lovers during the Depression doomed by their crimes. Keith Carradine and Shelley Duvall were excellent as the sympathetic characters searching for unattainable roots.*

Sexploitation characterized Big Bad Mama, *a film about sex-starved women terrorizing banks during the Depression. At left: William Shatner and Angie Dickinson.*

Left: although other black actors had been crimefighters, Richard Roundtree in Gordon Parks' Shaft was the first popular black private eye. He was praised by critics as an equal of Sam Spade and Philip Marlowe. Below: Ron O'Neal plays Youngblood Priest in Gordon Parks, Jr.'s Super Fly. Paradoxically, the tough, unsentimental drama drew criticism for creating new stereotypes and praise for its authenticity.

our society. Keith Carradine got top billing as a young inmate who escapes from a prison farm and joins up with small-time bank robbers. For them it is a way of life; for him only a means to something better with the girl (Shelley Duvall) he has fallen in love with. But the romance is doomed as the holdups lead to murders, friction among the gang members, and eventual tragedy. This deeply moving film admirably captured the life of lower-class people in the rural South. At the same time, it reflected today's cynical values.

Another important trend during the seventies was the black gangster film. Ossie Davis' *Cotton Comes to Harlem* started a boom in 1970. Faithful to the Chester Himes novel, the Davis Perl screenplay showed how Harlem police detectives Gravedigger Jones (Godfrey Cambridge) and Coffin Ed Johnson (Raymond St. Jacques) expose the crooked Reverend Deke O'Malley (Calvin Lockhart). Although not the first black gangster film, nor the first black-oriented production, it was the first successful black movie to chronicle crime in Harlem. Notable for its racial humor and appealing characters, the film's box-office success proved that black stars in gangster movies could be big money-makers.

Over the next three years dozens of white, traditional stories were adapted for black audiences. Gordon Parks' *Shaft* (1971) featured newcomer Richard Roundtree as a tough, no-nonsense black private eye fighting Harlem mobsters. Jack Starrett's *Slaughter* (1972) cast Jim Brown as a black ex-Green Beret in a vendetta against the Mafia. Barry Pollack's *Cool Breeze* (1972) was a remake of *The Asphalt Jungle*, with the crooks using Nixon and Agnew masks to pull off their million-dollar robbery. Larry Cohen's *Black Caesar* (1973) starred Fred Williamson as the black hustler who grew up to be just as ugly and vicious as his Mafia teachers.

The filmic highlight was *Super Fly,* in 1972, funded and produced entirely by blacks. Gordon Parks, Jr. made his directorial debut with a story about Priest (Ron O'Neal), a successful, black, New York cocaine dealer who wants to quit the racket—and does. Taking a compassionate view, screenwriter Phillip Feny revealed that the dealer was as much a victim of drugs as his pathetic users. The film's semidocumentary style and popularity created a storm of controversy. Those angered by the movie claimed it glorified dope peddling, and was one more in a line of films "representing black males as pimps, dope pushers, gangsters, and supermales, brimming with sexual prowess, but lacking any discernible skills." In defending *Super Fly*, O'Neal argued, "It portrays black people more intelligently than any other recent film made for blacks and should provoke a genuine sense of pride in the black community." One side effect of the debate was that within two years the black gangster was appearing less frequently on the screen.

Providing a balance to sympathetic stories about gangsters was the cop film. Its leading characters were independent policemen doing whatever was necessary to fight crime. Setting the pattern for the seventies was 1971's Oscar-winning film *The French Connection*.

One of the biggest box-office hits ever, *The French Connection* was based on a real-life event. In 1961, narcotics cops Eddie Egan and Sonny Grosso smashed a New York dope ring by seizing $32,000,000 worth of heroin. Robin Moore's best-selling novel about the case fascinated Philip D'Antoni, the producer of *Bullitt*. He hired the two cops as technical advisors to help director William Friedkin and screenwriter Ernest Tidyman create a thrilling, suspenseful movie. Adding to the gripping cops-and-robbers plot were brilliantly filmed chase sequences. Enthusiastic audiences ignored the fact that the movie cops (Gene Hackman and Roy Scheider) often broke the law in tracking down the dope peddlers, or that the film made a case for police brutality. So popular was *The French Connection* that the Motion Picture Academy gave it more Oscars than any other movie in 1971: best film, actor (Hackman), director, screenplay, editing (Jerry Greenberg).

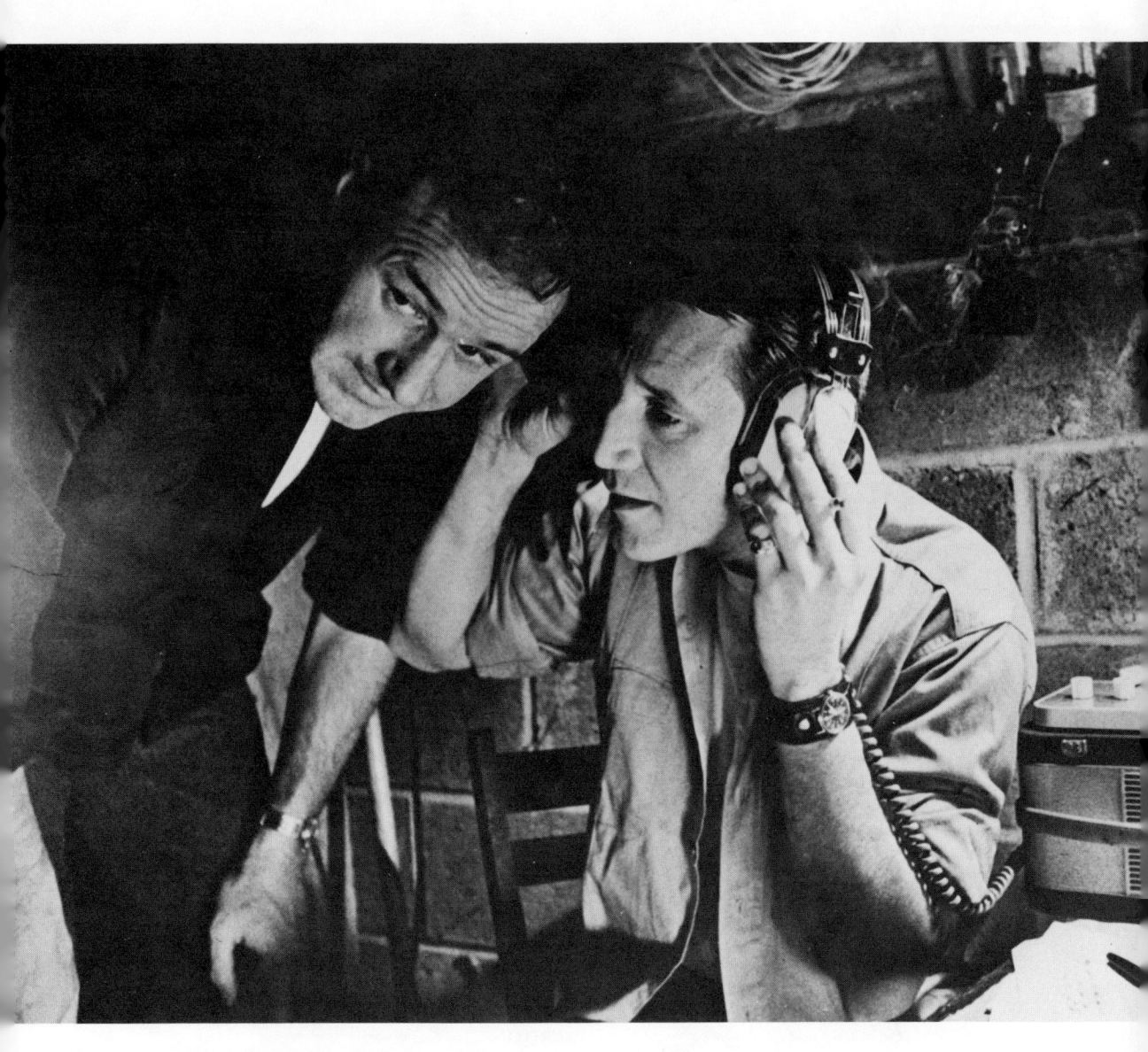

Gene Hackman (left), who won an Oscar for his acting, and Roy Scheider, as policemen, try to smash a big drug ring in William Friedkin's The French Connection. *The Academy Award-winning film was the model for future cop movies.*

Robert Blake plays Tony Baretta, an undercover cop who is a master of disguises and unique methods. Each week on Baretta, the street-wise law man gets help from drunks, pimps, or prostitutes who populate the hero's world.

Film-makers wasted no time in jumping on the bandwagon. Producer-director Don Siegel's *Dirty Harry* (1972) starred Clint Eastwood as a rogue cop determined to get his man. The reactionary plot attacked liberal values that allegedly protect criminals and endanger policemen. Director Richard Fleischer's *The New Centurions* (1972) turned the gritty novel by Los Angeles Sgt. Joseph Wambaugh into a police recruiting film. George C. Scott played a self-righteous veteran cop who shows rookie Stacy Keach that ghetto problems get solved by strong-arm tactics. Sidney Lumet's *Serpico* (1973) proved to be far more critical of policemen. Based on the real-life experiences of New York City detective Frank Serpico, who blew the whistle on police corruption, the Waldo Salt–Norman Wexler screenplay was dynamite. Al Pacino portrayed Serpico as the lone-wolf cop who desperately tries to reform the men in blue. But the film's critics attacked Lumet for exaggerating the problem, arguing his approach was no more honest than Fleischer's.

Supercops also showed up regularly on television. Exposing crime became routine business for Starsky and Hutch (David Soul and Paul Michael Glaser), Baretta (Robert Blake), Kojak (Telly Savalas), Police Woman Sergeant Pepper (Angie Dickinson), Columbo (Peter Falk), McCloud (Dennis Weaver), and San Francisco's ace detectives, Mike Stone (Karl Malden) and Steve Keller (Michael Douglas). The shows publicized honest cops, each respecting training, experience, and the law itself.

Private eyes also proved popular television heroes. Viewer support got extended runs for "Cannon" (William Conrad), "Barnaby Jones" (Buddy Ebsen), "The Rockford Files" (James Garner), and "Switch"'s odd couple, Pete (Robert Wagner) and Mac (Eddie Albert). Like the supercops, the detectives had to fend off flying fists, bullets, and pursuing automobiles before justice triumphed.

Above: Paul Michael Glaser (left) portrays David Starsky, the wise-cracking partner of David Soul's more subdued Ken Hutchinson. As undercover cops, the two star in the violent TV series Starsky and Hutch. *Shown here, they pose as narcotics dealers using Lynne Marta to trap a big-time drug boss. Right: William Conrad became the first fat hero in video history. As Frank Cannon, gourmet detective, he ran, pursued, and outwitted tough criminals on the series* Cannon.

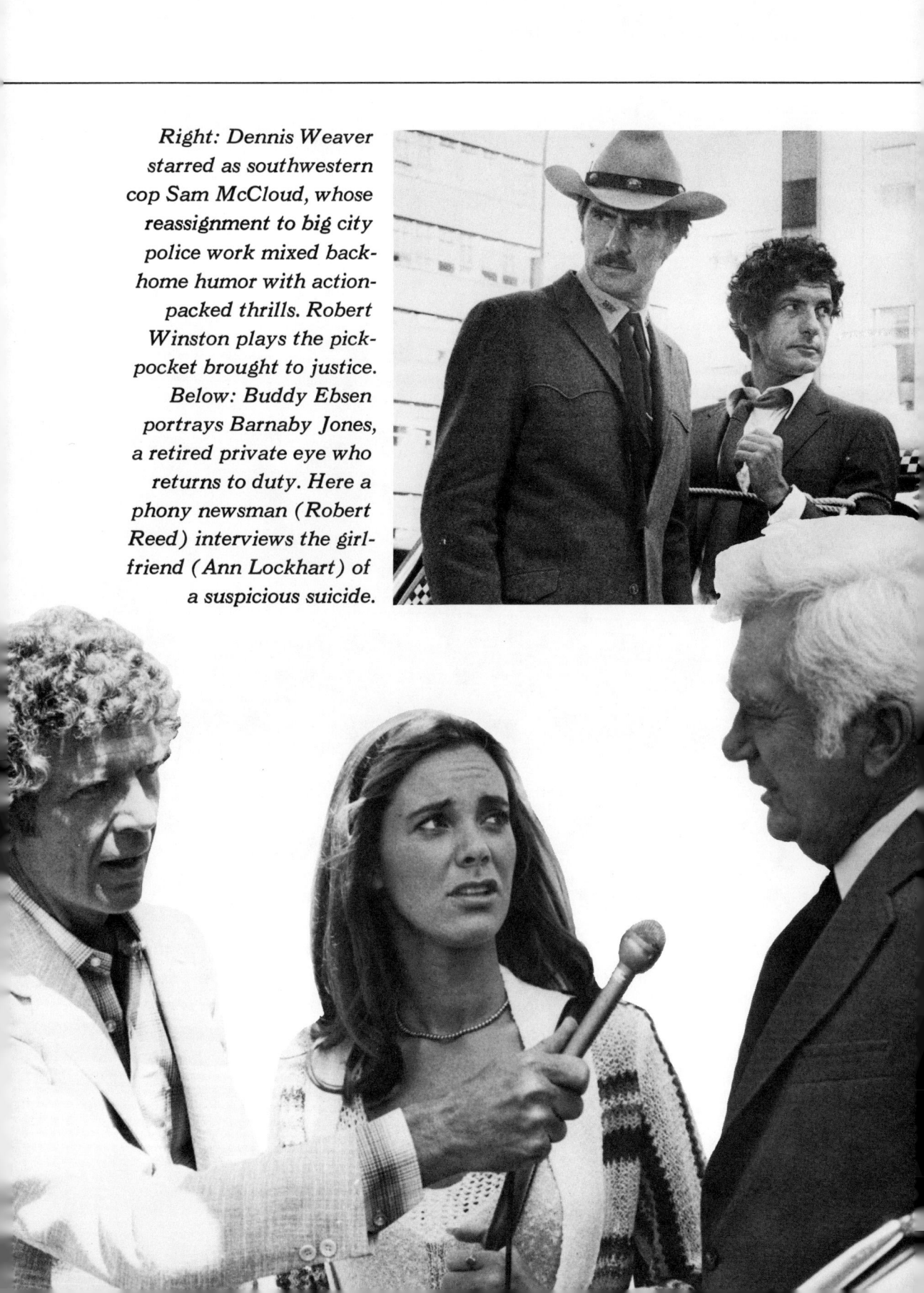

Right: Dennis Weaver starred as southwestern cop Sam McCloud, whose reassignment to big city police work mixed back-home humor with action-packed thrills. Robert Winston plays the pickpocket brought to justice. Below: Buddy Ebsen portrays Barnaby Jones, a retired private eye who returns to duty. Here a phony newsman (Robert Reed) interviews the girlfriend (Ann Lockhart) of a suspicious suicide.

Jack Nicholson played a Los Angeles detective who finds himself involved in political corruption and murder in Roman Polanski's much discussed Chinatown. *Repeated throughout the cynical film is the gag about a woman Nicholson once tried to help and only succeeded in destroying. The story was a foreshadowing of Faye Dunaway's future.*

Custodians of public morality were up in arms by the mid-seventies. Nothing seemed offensive to the mass audiences that put crime shows high on the TV ratings. To prove its point, a handful of citizens in Palo Alto, California, decided to publish a monthly newsletter entitled *Viewer's Disgust*, providing bloody statistics on prime-time shows and network films. Based on its system, the publishers reported in 1976, "a recent episode of 'Baretta' earned itself 1,119 points—one killing, one implied killing, seven attempted killings, and so on down the list to 29 references to killing. A *Streets of San Francisco* episode the same week was good for 1,061 points; *Police Story*, 690." As a result of such pressure from groups like *Viewer's Disgust,* the American Medical Association, the Parent-Teacher Association, and numerous religious organizations, the TV industry has switched its programming away from violent shows and towards situation comedies and musical revues. The danger is that in solving one problem the concerned citizens may have created another: unfair censorship. Who will decide now what is or is not necessary for an individual program?

In the meantime, competition from such violent crime serials forced film producers to find alternative material. The most striking example was Roman Polanski's *Chinatown* (1974).

Set in Los Angeles in 1937, *Chinatown* was, according to director Polanski, "a traditional detective story with a new and modern shape." The vintage elements centered around the Marlowe-like J. J. Gittes (Jack Nicholson) investigating top-drawer city government corruption and its predictable problems (coverups and murder). Decor and music carefully recreated the familiar thirties' conventions. Yet screenwriter Robert Towne modernized the formula with excessively violent scenes, perverted sexual relationships, and the feeling of helplessness. Critics loved the film even more than the mass audiences who made it one of the decade's big hits.

Despite the controversies and profits surrounding films like *The French Connection* and *Chinatown,* most viewers agreed that the major gangster films of the seventies were made by Francis Ford Coppola.

First came *The Godfather* in 1972. Billing it as "an Italian-American *Gone With the Wind,*" director Coppola compressed all the screen conventions of secret underworld societies into one panoramic epic. The film opens in 1945, when Don Vito Corleone (Marlon Brando) reigned as the head of one of the five families dominating organized crime in America. It detailed both his decline and the transformation of his youngest son, Michael (Al Pacino), from a decent World War II veteran into a merciless killer and eventually the Don's successor. Although violence reached new heights in the gripping melodrama, Coppola managed to elevate the gangster formula to a new plateau. Marvelously constructed scenes etched unforgettable images of the family's experiences: a daughter's wedding plagued by Mafia business, rival gangs struggling for power, assassinations galore, children corrupted not by greed but by tradition, murders for business not personal reasons. Equally impressive was the script's ability to link the methods of organized crime to those of large corporations and governments. It was a position best stated in an interview by Brando himself. "I don't think the film is about the Mafia at all," he explained. "I think it is about the corporate mind. In a way, the Mafia is the best example of capitalists we have. Don Corleone is just any ordinary American business magnate who is trying to do the best he can for the group he represents and for his family." Coppola also had the benefit of a splendid cast, which, besides Brando and Pacino, included James Caan, Richard Castellano, Robert Duvall, Sterling Hayden, Richard Conte, Diane Keaton, Al Lettieri, Abe Vigoda, and Talia Shire. Hailed as a classic around the world, *The Godfather* won Oscars for 1972's best film, actor (Brando), and screenplay adaptation.

Offered a contract he couldn't refuse, Coppola set out to

Francis Ford Coppola's The Godfather *offered a behind-the-scenes look at the fictional Corleone family, which became one of five groups heading organized crime. Marlon Brando starred as Don Corleone.*

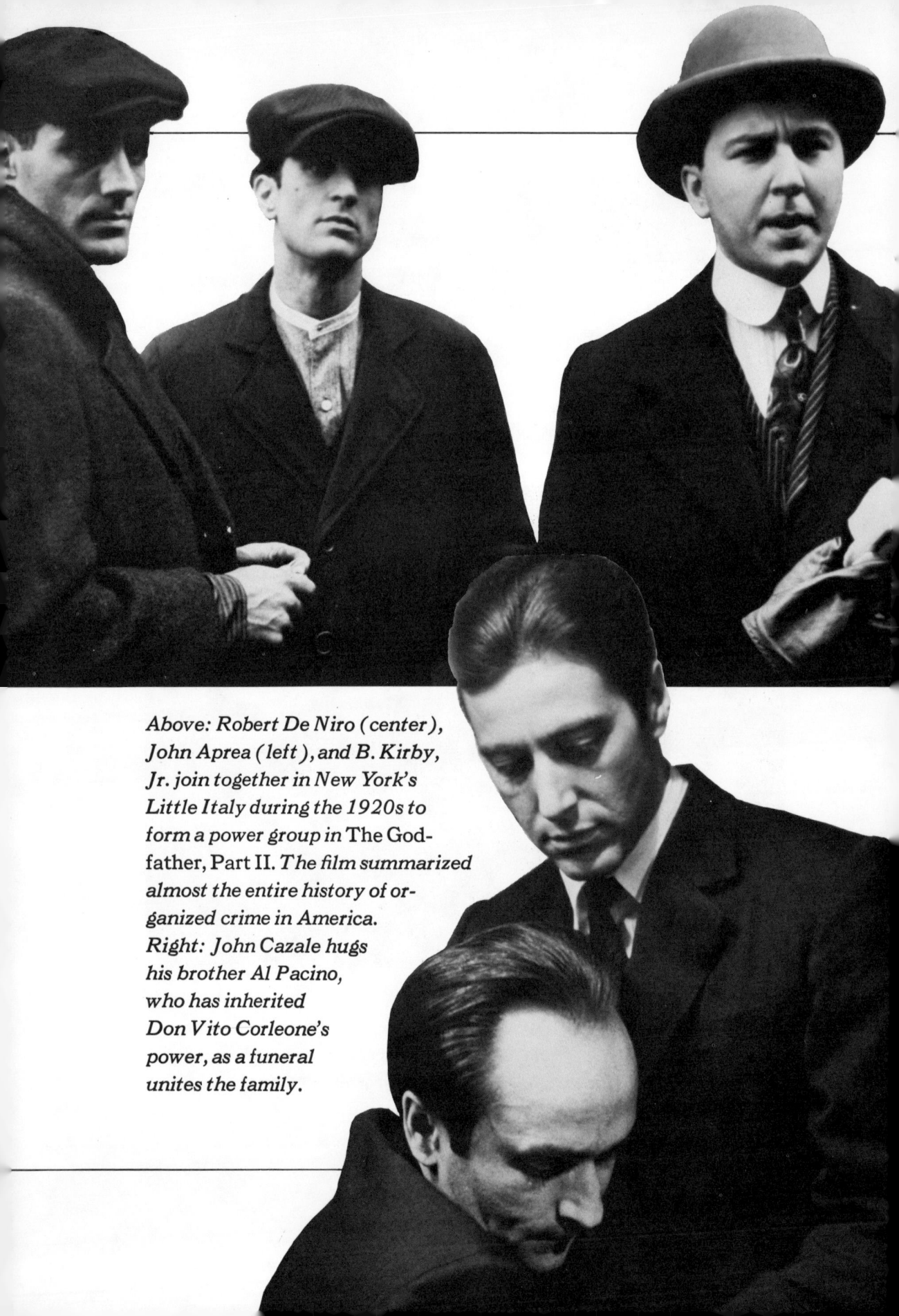

Above: Robert De Niro (center), John Aprea (left), and B. Kirby, Jr. join together in New York's Little Italy during the 1920s to form a power group in The Godfather, Part II. *The film summarized almost the entire history of organized crime in America. Right: John Cazale hugs his brother Al Pacino, who has inherited Don Vito Corleone's power, as a funeral unites the family.*

do what had never been done before—make a sequel to a movie that was better than the original. Other recent attempts to capitalize on films like *The French Connection, Shaft, Super Fly,* and *Dirty Harry* had all failed.

Then came *The Godfather, Part II* in 1974. Again Coppola coscripted the story with Mario Puzo (author of the best-selling novel). This time the Corleone chronicle traced three generations of the family's rise to power. Moving back and forth in time we discover why the young Don Vito (played by Robert De Niro instead of Brando) came to America, remained true to his Sicilian roots, and entered a life of crime. Contrasted with his father, Michael (Pacino) seems inhuman, concerned only with making money, and doomed to a lonely existence. If there were any doubts about Coppola's achievement, the 1974 Academy Awards tried to answer them by giving the sequel six Oscars, three more than the original: best picture, director, supporting actor (De Niro), art direction (Angelo Graham), screenplay adaptation, and original score (Nino Rota and Carmine Coppola).

Still not content, Coppola became part of a multimillion dollar deal to merge the two Oscar-winning films into a spectacular four-program television show, "The Godfather Saga." Carefully he began editing, cutting, and adding new scenes to what may well be the bloodiest, most violent television program ever shown. Late in 1977, the sensational feat hit the airways, with warnings from the network that parental caution was advised.

One only wonders what will come next as films and television compete in the violence derby for profits and fame. Nearly eighty years have passed since gangster films began to mirror American society. Yet people still debate the formula's effect on audiences. And as they search for answers, the public goes right on watching, enjoying, and honoring stories about organized crime. If there is one prediction possible, it is that the Hollywood gangster will never be any different from the society that breeds him.

BIBLIOGRAPHY

Alloway, Lawrence. *Violent America: The Movies 1946–1964*. New York: Museum of Modern Art, 1971.

Baxter, John. *The Gangster Film*. New York: A. S. Barnes, 1970.

Bogdanovich, Peter. *Fritz Lang in America*. New York: Praeger, 1976.

Clarens, Carlos. "Hooverville West: The Hollywood G-Man, 1934–1945," *Film Comment* 13:3 (May–June 1977), pp. 10–16.

Clark, Ramsey. *Crime in America: Observations on Its Nature, Cause, Prevention and Control*. New York: Pocket Books, 1971.

Davis, Brian. *The Thriller*. New York: Dutton, 1973.

Efron, Edith. "Does TV Violence Affect Our Society? No." *TV Guide* 23:24 (June 14, 1975), pp. 22–28.

Everson, William. *The Bad Guys: A Pictorial History of The Movie Villains*. New York: The Citadel Press, 1974.

———. *The Detective in Film*. New York: The Citadel Press, 1972.

Farber, Stephen. "The Bloody Movies: Why Film Violence Sells," *New York* 9:48 (November 29, 1976), pp. 39–45.

Gabree, John. *Gangsters*. New York: Pyramid, 1973.

Hickey, Neil. "Does TV Violence Affect Our Society? Yes." *TV Guide* 23:24 (June 14, 1975), pp. 8–17.

"Hollywood Fights Back: A Symposium on Sex and Violence," *TV Guide* 25:35 (August 27, 1977), pp. 4–18.

Jordan, René. *Marlon Brando*. New York: Pyramid, 1973.

Kagan, Norman. *The Cinema of Stanley Kubrick*. New York: Holt, Rinehart & Winston, 1972.

Karpf, Stephen. *The Gangster Film: Emergence, Variation and Decay of a Genre, 1930–1940*. New York: Arno Press, 1973.

Kiester, Edwin Jr. "*The Godfather* is Reborn," *TV Guide* 25:46 (November 12, 1977), pp. 4–8.

Lee, Raymond, and Van Hecke, B. C. *Gangsters and Hoodlums: The Underworld in the Cinema*. New York: A. S. Barnes, 1971.

McArthur, Colin. *Underworld USA*. New York: Viking Press, 1972.

McBride, Joseph. *Kirk Douglas*. New York: Pyramid, 1976.

Nash, Jay Robert. *Bloodletters and Badmen: Book II*. New York: Warner Books, 1973.

———. *Book III*. New York: Warner Books, 1975.

Nolan, William F. *John Huston: King Rebel*. Los Angeles: Sherbourne Press, 1965.

Parish, James Robert. *The Tough Guys*. New Rochelle: Arlington House, 1976.

Pendo, Stephen. *Raymond Chandler on Screen: His Novels into Films*. Metuchen, N.J.: The Scarecrow Press, 1976.

Rovin, Jeff. *The Great Television Series*. New York: A. S. Barnes, 1977.

Sherman, Eric, and Rubin, Martin. *The Director's Event*. New York: Atheneum, 1969.

Solomon, Stanley J. *Beyond Formula: American Film Genres*. New York: Harcourt Brace Jovanovich, 1976.

Wood, Robin. *Arthur Penn*. New York: Praeger, 1969.

INDEX

Al Capone, 82, 83
All Through the Night, 57
Altman, Robert, 98, 99, 101
Anastasia, Albert, 53
Angels with Dirty Faces, 48, 49, 51, 78
Asphalt Jungle, The, 72, 73, 74, 81, 101
Astor, Mary, 55, 56

Bacall, Lauren, 60, 61, 65, 66
Bancroft, George, 22, 23
"Baretta," 105, 109
Barker, "Ma," 43, 97, 98
Barrow, Clyde, 43, 89, 91
Barrymore, Lionel, 65, 66
Beatty, Warren, 89, 90, 91
Beery, Wallace, 28, 36
Big Bad Mama, 98, 99
Big Heat, The, 75, 77, 78
Big House, The, 28, 30, 71
Big Sleep, The, 60, 61, 62, 92
Birdman of Alcatraz, 87, 88
Black Hand, The, 12, 13

Blake, Robert, 104, 105
Bloody Mama, 97, 98
Bogart, Humphrey, 45, 46, 47, 48, 51, 54, 55, 56, 57, 60, 61, 65, 66, 74
Bonnie and Clyde, 88, 89, 90, 91, 92
Boorman, John, 92, 93, 94
Brackett, Leigh, 61
Brando, Marlon, 2, 79, 80, 83, 110, 111
Brotherhood, The, 94, 95
Brown, Jim, 94, 101
Brute Force, 62, 63
Buchalter, Louis "Lepke," 18, 37, 87
Bullets or Ballots, 46, 47
Bullitt, 92, 93, 94, 102
Burnett, W. R., 31, 53, 73

Caged, 71, 72, 73, 82
Cagney, James, 6, 29, 30, 33, 34, 35, 36, 40, 44, 46, 47, 49, 50, 51, 55, 68, 69, 97
Calhern, Louis, 72, 73, 74

"Cannon," 105
Capone, Al, 18, 20, 26, 39, 43, 82, 83, 88
Carradine, Keith, 99, 101
Censorship, 4, 7, 13, 20, 21, 40, 41, 48, 85, 95, 97, 109
Chandler, Raymond, 18, 61
Chinatown, 108, 109, 110
"Columbo," 105
Conrad, William, 105, 106
Conte, Richard, 65, 67
Coppola, Francis Ford, 110
Corman, Roger, 88, 97, 98
Cotton Comes to Harlem, 101
Criss Cross, 68
Cry of the City, 65, 67
Curtiz, Michael, 51

Dead End, 48
Dead End Kids, 48, 51
Dickinson, Angie, 5, 92, 98, 99, 105
Dillinger, 1, 98
Dillinger, John, 43, 55, 61, 68
Dirty Harry, 105, 113
Doorway to Hell, The, 29, 30, 37
Douglas, Kirk, 94, 95
"Dragnet," 74
Dunaway, Faye, 90, 91, 108
Duvall, Shelley, 99, 101

Enforcer, The, 74
Eviction, The, 13
Ex-Convict, The, 13

Falk, Peter, 5, 86, 87, 105
Farewell, My Lovely, 61
Fatal Hour, The, 13
Faulkner, William, 61
Film Noir, 56, 57, 61, 62, 78
Floyd, "Pretty Boy," 43, 82, 98
Force of Evil, 67, 78
Frankenheimer, John, 87, 88
French Connection, The, 102, 103, 110, 113
Friedkin, William, 102, 103
Fuller, Sam, 74, 87

Gable, Clark, 36, 37
Garfield, John, 67
Genovese, Vito, 28
George, Gladys, 50, 56
Glaser, Paul Michael, 105
G-Men, 44, 46
Godfather, The, 1, 2, 3, 7, 110, 111
Godfather, Part II, The, 2, 112, 113
Gomez, Thomas, 65, 66
Greenstreet, Sydney, 56, 61
Griffith, D. W., 14, 15, 16, 17
Guardino, Harry, 92, 93

Hackman, Gene, 89, 102, 103
Hammett, Dashiel, 18, 55, 61
Harlow, Jean, 33, 36, 37
Hawks, Howard, 39, 40, 61

Hays, Will H., 20, 26, 40, 41, 61
Hayward, Susan, 81, 82
Hecht, Ben, 23, 39, 64
Hellinger, Mark, 62, 63
Heroes of the Street, 19
He Walked By Night, 74
High Sierra, 53, 54, 55, 69, 73
Hill, George, 28, 36, 37
Hoover, J. Edgar, 43, 44, 53
Howard, Leslie, 45, 47
Hughes, Howard, 26, 39, 40
Huston, John, 53, 55, 56, 65, 73, 74

Intolerance, 16, 17
I Want to Live, 81, 82

Karloff, Boris, 39, 40
Karlson, Phil, 80, 88
Kazan, Elia, 78, 79, 80
Kefauver, Estes, 74
Keighley, William, 44, 47
Kellogg, Virginia, 68, 73
Kelly, "Machine Gun," 43, 44, 82, 98
Key Largo, 65, 66
Killers, The, 62, 63, 88
Killing, The, 81
Kiss Me Deadly, 80
Kiss of Death, 64
"Kojak," 1, 3, 7, 105
Kubrick, Stanley, 81

Ladd, Alan, 58, 59
Lady in the Lake, 61

Lake, Veronica, 58, 59
Lancaster, Burt, 62, 63, 68, 88
Lang, Fritz, 63, 75, 76, 77
Lansky, Meyer, 18
LeRoy, Mervyn, 31, 32
Lindbergh, Charles, 41, 43
Little Caesar, 6, 31, 32, 35, 38, 39, 40, 48, 51, 73
Long Goodbye, The, 61
Lorre, Peter, 56, 57, 61
Luciano, Charles "Lucky," 18, 28, 38, 53, 58
Lumet, Sidney, 105
Lupino, Ida, 54

MacLane, Barton, 46, 56
Madigan, 92, 93, 94
Mafia, 12, 20, 38, 58, 74, 86, 94, 101, 110, 113
Malden, Karl, 79, 105
Maltese Falcon, The, 55, 56, 61
Marion, Frances, 28, 36, 37
Marvin, Lee, 77, 92, 93
Mature, Victor, 65
Mayo, Archie, 29, 44
McClellan, John, 82
"McCloud," 105
McQueen, Steve, 92, 93
Milestone, Lewis, 24, 26
Monroe, Marilyn, 72, 73
Montgomery, Robert, 28, 30
Moorehead, Agnes, 72, 73
Moran, Bugs, 88
Moran, Eugene, 18
Muni, Paul, 39, 40, 47

Murder, Inc., 86, 87
"Murder, Inc.," 53, 74
Musketeers of Pig Alley, The, 14, 15

Nicholson, Jack, 108, 109
Niro, Robert De, 112, 113

Oates, Warren, 1, 98
O'Brien, Edmond, 62
O'Brien, Pat, 51
O'Neal, Ron, 100, 101, 102
On The Waterfront, 78, 79, 80, 81
Organized crime, 10, 11, 18, 26, 28, 37, 38, 43, 53, 74, 78, 82, 87, 94, 110, 113

Pacino, Al, 2, 105, 110, 112, 113
Parker, Bonnie, 43, 82, 89, 91
Parker, Eleanor, 71, 72
Parks, Gordon, 100
Parks, Gordon, Jr., 101
Penalty, The, 19
Penn, Arthur, 89, 90, 91, 98
Peters, Jean, 74, 76
Petrified Forest, The, 44, 45, 65
Phenix City Story, The, 80
Pickup on South Street, 74, 76, 78, 87
Point Blank, 92, 93, 94
Polanski, Roman, 108, 109
"Police Story," 4, 109
"Police Woman," 4, 105

Prohibition, 17, 18, 19, 26, 29, 33, 37, 41, 51, 58, 74
Public Enemy, The, 6, 32, 33, 34, 35, 38, 39, 40, 74

Racket, The, 24, 26
Raft, George, 39, 40, 47, 55
Rags to Riches, 20, 21
Reles, Abe "Kid Twist," 53, 86, 87
Revenge, 12
Riot in Cell Block 11, 78, 79
Rise and Fall of "Legs" Diamond, The, 85, 86
Ritt, Martin, 94, 95
Roaring Twenties, The, 50, 51
Robinson, Edward G., 6, 31, 32, 35, 36, 40, 46, 47, 48, 51, 55, 65, 97
Rochemont, Louis De, 61, 64
"Rockford Files, The," 105
Rounding Up of the "Yeggmen," 10
Roundtree, Richard, 100, 101

St. Valentine's Day Massacre, The, 88
Saint, Eva Marie, 79, 80
Savalas, Telly, 105
Scarface, 39
Scheider, Roy, 102, 103
Schulberg, Budd, 50, 78
Schultz, Dutch, 18, 37, 48
Secret Six, The, 36, 37

Serpico, 105
Shaft, 100, 101, 113
Shannon, Cleo, 43, 44
Sherwood, Robert, 45
Siegel, Benjamin "Bugsy," 53
Siegel, Don, 78, 79, 82, 88, 92, 105
Siodmak, Robert, 63, 65, 67, 68
Slight Case of Murder, A, 51
Soul, David, 105, 106
Split, The, 94
"Starsky and Hutch," 105, 106
Sternberg, Josef von, 22, 23
Street of Forgotten Men, The, 20
Street with No Name, The, 64
"Streets of San Francisco," 109
Super Fly, 7, 101, 102, 113
Syndicate, The, 38, 53, 74, 78, 86, 87, 94

They Live by Night, 98
Thieves Like Us, 98, 99, 101
This Gun for Hire, 58, 59

Traffic in Souls, 14
Trevor, Claire, 48, 65
Turkus, Burton, 53, 87

Underworld, 22, 23
Underworld, U.S.A., 86, 87
Untouchables, The, 37, 82

Valachi Papers, The, 1, 7
Violence, 1, 3, 4, 7, 11, 14, 26, 78, 82, 85, 91, 92, 97, 113

Walsh, Raoul, 51, 53, 68, 69
Warner Brothers, 29, 44, 51
Weaver, Dennis, 105, 107
Webb, Jack, 74
White Heat, 68, 69, 81
Widmark, Richard, 64, 74, 76, 92, 93
Wilder, Billy, 63
Wilson, Richard, 82, 83, 86
Wise, Robert, 81, 82
Woods, Edward, 33, 34
Wycherly, Margaret, 68, 69
Wyler, William, 48
Wynn, Keenan, 92, 93

Yates, Peter, 92